STANDUP

An RV Journey into Financial Freedom, Personal Development

… and the Meaning of It All

Genti Cici

Publishing Information

Copyright© 2020 Genti Cici

All Rights Reserved.

No part of this book may be reproduced in any form or by any electronic means, without written permission from the author. The sole exception is for the use of brief quotations in a book review. The unauthorized reproduction or distribution of this copyrighted work is illegal.

Table of Contents

Publishing Information	2
Table of Contents	3
Acknowledgements	4
Introduction	5
Chapter 1: What's Wrong?	7
Chapter 2: From Fear to Fearless	23
Chapter 3: On a Mission	37
Chapter 4: Be Greedy (Not What You're Thinking)	55
Chapter 5: How to Get it All?	65
Chapter 6: Planning's at the Core	75
Chapter 7: Budgeting, Net Worth & Debt Management	85
Chapter 8: Retirement Savings	105
Chapter 9: Investment Strategies & Common Mistakes	119
Chapter 10: The Rest of Financial Planning	149
Chapter 11: All about RVing	177
Chapter 12: What's Next?	205

Acknowledgements

I'd first like to thank my wife for being such a great copilot on this trip, a spiritual copilot and motivator, but also an *actual* copilot and navigator.

She didn't automatically say NO to a crazy idea of RVing around the country that I brought to her one random day. Instead, she became even a further motivator on the trip that we'll always remember.

Next, I'd like to thank all my family and friends who were supportive and motivational as well, making me feel better in a time full of doubts.

Thank you—just thank you—to all of you.

And may all of your trips—financial and global—turn out great.

Introduction

This book is about freedom—the freedom to be you, the freedom to live your life to the fullest, and the freedom to achieve both of these things via a host of practical, 'road-tested' ideas and supported by lots of financial planning tips, actions & recommendations.

I'm a Certified Financial Planner (CFP®) by trade and an amateur thinker by nature. So, I wonder, ask questions, and even answer some of them—and leave the rest to be answered by you. In this book, we'll delve deep into the *Why's*: Why we do this thing vs. another thing, Why we bother to wake up in the morning (besides our internal clocking telling us to do so) and how to find what we're good at.

And finally, we look at a *What*: what to really do about it.

During these fifteen months of an unconventional RV trip & business venture, I've had a lot of time to slow down, wonder and ask more questions than I've found answers to, but that's the beginning of it for all of us.

In this ever-fast world of interconnectivity, social media, politics, money, media and more, there's pretty much no time for our own thoughts. They get crowded and pushed away by the so-called experts on TV or social media.

We're not really thinking anymore; we're all just floating, and the tide is taking us here and there, once left, then right, then up or down. Without knowing what to do or believe, we get even closer to our comfort zone, to ideas and people we agree with, at the exact time that we need to get out and get a breath of fresh air, a new perspective, slowing down time, our thinking, our actions and our reactions.

It is in this semi-relaxed state of slowed-down reality where we can try to detach and look at everything around us as 'visitors from another planet, place and time' and ask and challenge all that we do in here.

It is at this point that we can try to see what's happening, why we are here, doing what we're doing—and we can challenge most of it.

In fact, I lived in this semi-relaxed state for fifteen months, living full-time in an RV while traveling tens of thousands of miles around all of the US.

This is my story of what I felt, how I saw it and what I'm doing about it. Hopefully, it will provide some inspiration for your own internal trip around your mind and maybe provide you a road map that can help you on that trip. As a Certified Financial Planner, this book is also filled with practical actions and ideas on how to take control of your financial life, while using those resources toward your goals, ambitions and destiny.

Last, this book may make you feel flustered at times, in total disagreement and even angry with me. And that's totally fine; that's a normal reaction to (maybe) different viewpoints to which we're not accustomed yet, and especially if they challenge old-world beliefs that we hold so dearly. On the other hand, if you can read it even while you're disagreeing with it, it is said—by known 20th century author F. Scott Fitzgerald—that holding two opposing views at the same time is healthy for your mind and a test of 'first-rate intelligence'. So, as you've been properly warned, you can now enter.

Chapter 1

What's Wrong?

So, I'm thinking about being different...

What are you talking about? How can you 'think' about being different? I hear you say.

And that's true, mostly.
You don't 'think' about it; you just are. You know it and feel it—so no, you don't 'think it'. Yes, hi, hello. Please sit down, take a breath, have a cup of water – I was expecting your reaction to the above.

Please sit down, please.

First, welcome. I promise you'll have lots of ups and downs in this book, moments where your heart will race fast enough that you'd want to skip gym for the day. Secondly, the reason you came up here, running and out of breath to tell me that I'm wrong is that is all we do nowadays. Who hasn't heard the meme:

'Honey, come to bed.'

You: 'Wait, not yet, someone is wrong on the Internet'.

We become so entangled in this fast-paced world that our reactions are fast too, and I used a 'disagreement trick' to bring you in this room. You're sitting on a red couch, and you can feel the supple leather; touch it, go ahead.

Slow your breathing and read with me for a moment.

Now, yes, you're right. We don't 'think' to be different – we just are, and we know about it and feel it inside. But the thinking part comes when communicating it to the world. Would you like to share it with them or keep it inside of you? If you don't share it with anyone, is it even real?

For many people in the US, just saying my name is different. It's just five letters—Genti—and yet I already get 3-4 different pronunciations, including the 'I give up, I'll call you G'. But my name is just the beginning. My name is not the hard part.

I was born in Eastern Europe, Albania, under one of the harshest communist regimes of the era, only similar to current North Korea. No, we didn't have nukes and it's now a democracy where we're free to come and go, but it wasn't like that before 1990.

Freedom was a word just in history books, and primarily talked about how we won the war over the Nazis in WWII.

And that was the end of the word 'Freedom' for many Albanians at that time.

The Bread Line

At that time, I didn't understand, but I endured bread lines, which for many that don't know, are not just for bread. We also had meat lines, chicken lines, milk lines and many other lines of scarce resources. Not to give a lesson in communism here, but at the end of life of communism, resources get scarcer and lines even longer.

I remember waiting in line outside of the store because of just a rumor that the product would be there sometime that day; of course, it never came. You could say it was just like at an Apple Store nowadays, where everyone queues for a new iPhone release, but the communists at that time were not that punctual. I remember my brother and I taking turns waiting 3-4 hours each, then getting to be among the top five in line and the product running out—and I recall how we went home after eight hours with nothing to show for it. Sometimes, when our staying-in-line venture worked out, my brother and I would even eat our way through half of the product before bringing it home, and blame it on the seller for not giving us enough cheese or salami or whatever.

That didn't work well most often, but we wanted compensation for our efforts, I guess. Perhaps, even in those early days, my mind was already thinking of rewards.

No wonder, then, that I was to become a financial planner.

One of the top stories of something that happened to me during that time was when I was again in a long bread line. Being just eleven or twelve years old, I was wearing open shoes—which I now know is a mistake for waiting in lines, all you Apple Store in-line waiters. Anyway, I finally reached the counter, but imagine a line where everyone is 'first' next to a ten-foot long counter and then you have seven or eight rows of people behind you, all pushing and shoving to get through to the front.

Well, the problem with that system is that it isn't a system at all; it is chaos at best, created by the notion of scarcity and the knowledge that there's only enough bread for just 25% of the people waiting. And that's on a good day.

The problem with that system—pretty obvious, isn't it?—is that there's no room to get out, first, if you even want to for any reason *before* getting the bread, and second if you've got the bread and now want to make off with it safely and head homeward.

So, what do you do?

More importantly, what if you have never experienced that before?

For me it was a first in terms of experiencing that level of pushing, feeling the weight of so many people behind me and of a counter that was 'cutting me to my stomach'.

It was getting unbearable.

So, I would ask the person next to me or behind me to let me go, but he would just give a look that said, wordlessly, that he was stuck there too, pressed in turn by the five or six rows of people all thronging behind him.

But intuition and self-preservation kicked in, weighted down by an enormous sense of guilt that I was silently realizing the only way to get free of the pushing was when all the bread ran out. I could almost pray for it to happen... The pain was so, so bad.

I did a quick eye exchange with the seller, indicating that I was about to do something she wouldn't like. So, I decided to climb the counter, and then buy the bread while atop it. The bread, admittedly, was now secondary, and my pain level so high that I couldn't breathe. I pushed a bit back to make room and climbed over the counter, coming to crouch there on the corner of it. The clerk, as expected, yelled at me, but I pointed to the crowd with a look that said it was now too late and anyway, I'd had no other choice.

Oh, almost forgot about the relevance of those open shoes.

I'll say it again. Never, ever wear un-laced shoes to a bread line, ever.

Climbing up, I had to coordinate getting myself, being squeezed hard as I climbed while holding tight the shoes that were about to come off. Not a good circus position. After 5-10 minutes, my wicked prayers were answered and the bread ran out, the crowd dispersed and I could now come down from atop the corner of the counter.

I say thank you to the shopkeeper—a government employee, for those of you that don't know—and I could continue home.

This story and similar ones may seem completely out of place and irrelevant in developed countries such as the US where I now live. But I disagree, and I'll be bringing many more stories to bring home many points in this book.

So, get ready for those. And I'm sure that by the time we reach the end of this book, you'll have thought of a few of your own.

Back to what we were talking about; this story was about deciding to be different, and how—yes, relax, now—we don't *think* about being different, but we just are.

I didn't choose to be born there or to be there at that bread line; it just happened.

But most often, we don't think about how these experiences affect us, the subconscious and conscious change it leaves in us. So, thinking about being different is about recognizing your differences, acknowledging them and using them to form you, to better you, to guide you. That's the thinking part of it. You *are* different, you just are, but we have to think about how to express it all to ourselves first—what we learned/will learn from it and how to move forward.

These past experiences are ingrained in you, just like your fingerprints and your DNA, and many more lessons can be learned that will help facilitate your future.

So, back to bread lines specifically—or any lines or public gathering for that matter. The lesson here is to not be in one. And if you have to be in one for reasons beyond your control, make sure you have a planned way out. My way out was climbing, while my brother's was pushing back at the counter like a jumper on a trampoline and exploding backwards with four or five other people carried along as well, all now angry at him as they lost their place in line.

Pyramid Schemes

Coming to the US at neither a young enough age to become completely assimilated or to have no accent, nor old enough to feel completely outside of it, I came into the country when just seventeen years old. I'd left Albania after one of the harshest lawlessness experiences of 1997, after most Albanians had just lost all their savings in the pyramid schemes of the mid-1990s. Now, I see it was my first encounter with 'investing'.

Although, as we now know, fraud and pyramid schemes aren't anything like real investing at all, but then, coming out of communism, our understanding of anything that was not state property was very slim. So, a pyramid scheme looked really like a tempting way to invest. We also had no idea of what might constitute a reasonable investment return, and it seemed like 200% returns over a three-month period—as some of the schemes were paying that much toward the end of their lives—must be just about right, since all the supposedly 'safe & sound' investment firms were paying such.

Now, after many years, I realize that what happened would have never come to pass if we'd had even a slim knowledge of financial literacy.

Many people sold their homes or livestock to invest in such schemes, and many immigrants brought money back to Albania to invest in them. And then when all was lost, anger built and built until finally, it exploded. For a period of 3-4 days, complete lawlessness reigned—which continued on to 'limited' lawlessness for months afterward, with police leaving their stations, jails breaking wide open and military personnel deserting their installations, that all got completely ravaged and emptied out of most of their weapons and ammo. Kids no older than twelve or thirteen were seen carrying AK47s on the streets, showing off their newly acquired toys, total chaos brought about by the collapse of the pyramid schemes that had defrauded most of the hard-working Albanians. While many may think that this is in the past, I believe many people acquired untreated PTSD due to this inexplicable and unimaginable event occurring in any developed country. And probably, I do too. Fear and helplessness get deep into your soul and believe that they can stay there permanently.

If you don't work on that, they will become permanent.

Now in the US, and after being here for a while with an MBA in Finance, different investment accreditations, experience under my belt and great connections, family and friends, I was thinking (again) about 'being different'. This time, I wanted to be different with a purpose, with a mission larger than myself and looking toward making a change for others. But what could I give or do? The cravings to find meaning & purpose in life were my answer to myself.

'*RVing and doing Financial Literacy Events, helping others, and building a business*' comprised my new way of being different. But there were too many people who either openly couldn't see it and expressed it to me, or who secretly thought, 'Why do this?' 'What is this RV thing?', and 'Well, where will you be going, staying, sleeping?'

My mindset was different.

Other people's mindsets were all the same.

My differences were just too radical for most, who craved familiarity and believed that doing things the same way day after day for the rest of your life was what gave stability and security. Without sameness, things would surely fall apart.

But are you sure? Doubts—leading to self-doubts

Whenever you think differently from most folks and want to do something about it, there are always doubts. Many are self-doubts, about whether you're doing the right thing—if that's the right path to choose or whether it's the right time. And what's worse is that many of these doubts are not even your own; they are helpfully introduced to you by other people. When you set out to think differently or do something 'other' than what the majority do, people will think you have lost the plot.

Friends and relatives will doubt your ideas too, maybe suggesting you think again or change an aspect of your plan, or sometimes maybe even foist their thoughts onto you. That definitely doesn't make it easier when you see them exchanging knowing glances, but you can overcome it.

Also, I should note here that most of your family and friends will mean well when they express their reservations about something that's not common. It comes from a place of love and care, but also from a place of tradition, norms and customs. It will also come from fear of the unknown, of breaking new territory. So, they mean well.

But just because it's well-intended doesn't make it easier on you.

Most of us who are thinking about doing or being something different already have their own self-doubts, and if we have to add on the burden of family members' and friends' doubts, it makes it even harder to progress—to get on and do it. It's like setting off on a trip with just a carry-on bag and then all your relatives pile on their three sets of 30kg wheeled baggage that you're supposed to carry along too.

Luckily, my personal experience was actually much better, with family & friends turning out to be more accepting than I'd thought—or so it seemed, as I followed certain steps to minimize my own self-doubt as well as others' input. As you'll notice below, we used few and simple steps to reduce doubt and to prepare, and these steps can be used for any new (and different) initiative you'd like to undertake, not just full-time RVing.

A few steps to reduce doubts and move forward

Here are a handful of practical steps you can take to shake off those doubts and ensure you can progress with your plans.

1. Have goals

Have a clear goal for what you're doing, as well as a 'Why?'

For me, my goal was to travel around the US, reaching out to all universities and colleges and offering free financial literacy to promote young people's knowledge about money and how to align it with their goals. I also wanted to motivate people with the main reason of why I'd give up some of 'today's fun' in favor of 'tomorrow's security'. My 'Why?' for doing this was that I felt obligated, at least morally to share my knowledge with people, help them out with their money concerns so it could liberate them to do other worthwhile ventures. Money, while it has a negative connotation, can give you the freedom to do things you really enjoy, to be creative and thoughtful, and eventually to use your time to help yourself and others. You just have to know how to use money appropriately.

2. **Plan for your worst-case scenario**

This may sound crazy and very negative—but for me, it was key in my analysis and plans. If you have a plan for what could go wrong and how you will cope with that, you won't get caught out. Now, of course, you can come up with really worst-case scenarios, including death, but that's not what I mean here. There are definitely risks to being on the road, RVing around the country and sleeping in who-knows-where, so the worst case scenario I mainly thought of and for which I built a strategy—and remember, this was about my *own* goal and situation, so yours will differ—was in regard to personal safety and money. Ask yourself, *can we survive typical (or some even atypical) events on the road, and will we be ok financially even if we have no clients or make no money by the time we end this?* If the answer is YES to both, then you pass the test. We passed our 'worst case scenario' test.

3. **List the positives**

Now, that the worst is over, think about what positives you'll reach or experience from your venture. For us, it was a (probably) once-in-a-lifetime experience, RVing around the US, visiting all the states, checking national parks and local areas, and sharing financial literacy with as many people as we could. Just the excitement in our eyes was enough to really know we were up for a great experience.

4. **Plan for it, but don't try to be 100% ready**

You'll never be, and if waiting for that, you'll never do it. In fact, you're probably using 'being ready' as an excuse. If you're forever coming up with what-ifs and having to add more and more to your preparations, you need to ask yourself if you are really committed to doing it.

There's a certain degree of preparedness that makes sense. But it's a little like anticipating a great natural disaster; you can never really know just how many cans of soup you'll need in the event of getting stuck at home in quarantine or lockdown, so just buy a sensible stock (metaphorically—I am not suggesting you go buying soup) and then *make it happen*. Whatever 'it' is. So, not waiting until you are 100% ready is about preparedness without overkill.

5. Tell others only when the time has come

Now, here, depends who you consider 'others'. If someone is doing this with you or you believe s/he will be a motivator and a helper in your initiative, you may want to share earlier and also get help from that person. If s/he can help, share it earlier, if s/he cannot really help, it can wait.

The point of this is that the nearer you get toward your starting point and the less exposure you have to others' influence—when they try to give you all those helpful hints and pieces of advice that just are determined to dissuade you—the more likely you'll say *thanks, but I am doing it anyway*. In the early stages, you could be put off or end up overcomplicating things by telling anyone.

6. Set the timeline and go

Just go and do it. Overthinking won't help you and will probably paralyze you. If you've got most of the angles covered, you are ready.

What's Wrong?

You don't need to have everything nailed down; you'll find out some as you go, and other things cannot even be known in advance. What's the point on dwelling and worrying about it?

I started this chapter with people asking you, 'What's wrong?' when you express a different idea about something that falls outside their comfort zone.

Just to get the record straight, I've used the word 'different' and haven't said 'better', as we just don't know that yet. Very few 'different' ideas are better just by design.

For your new and 'different' idea to also be 'better', it means that it is much better than all the existing ideas, including the current 'best idea'.

And that is a hard feat by design, but not impossible. If that were the case—impossible—then we would never innovate or aim to do better.

But very often, innovation cannot find its home inside comfort, the known and expected. In order to find innovation and think differently, you need a fresh environment, something unique and unexpected. You'll see things from a new perspective, and for me, it was RVing that gave me this. Leaving the comforts of home behind and getting inside a 'home' with wheels, being anywhere and nowhere at the same time, having the time to drive, think or just be and daydream, gave me much-needed new perspective.

Sometimes, you have to get out to see in.

Are you a prepper? The subconscious prep...

No, I don't mean the Doomsday Preppers. But something this big, like quitting your job to get in an RV and travel the country for at least a year while doing financial literacy seminars doesn't just happen overnight, even for a spontaneous mind like myself. For me, ideas come, stay a while, and if I don't entertain them, they just go. Many ideas are somewhere in the trashcan folder of my mind, somewhat upset at me that I didn't entertain or play with them longer. Everyone operates differently, but for myself, I have to continue entertaining the idea and keep it alive for a while, but not for too long to fall in the category of 'overthinking'.

Sometimes, the idea comes disguised as something else or the result is not what the original idea was for. This idea of RVing didn't come like that either. It came in search of alternative ways to operate, more freedom to do things I liked to do, research, dream and come up with solutions. This came as a personal and financial freedom idea, allowing one to live simpler, cover all our expenses and then have the time to wander and create and innovate. Most often, I don't remember how I stumble through things and arrive where I do. But I do remember this one came from research on the 'tiny house' movement, people who had found their freedom by not choosing to lock themselves up with a thirty-year mortgage, living very simply in beautiful areas and appreciating their time on this earth.

It came as a look for freedom from the typical work-home-work cycle where many people are miserable doing what they do, hating their jobs and their environment but staying in it due to their financial needs and the need to pay their bills. RVing was a derivation of that idea, as well as a taster of the tiny house lifestyle.

This idea and derivations of it came to me at least three months before I shared it with my wife. It was coming and going, but never really left. Not sure how others operate, but for me, after liking an idea, I entertain versions of it and potentially, a lot of the prepping is happening subconsciously. When I jump into something, it's not really that spontaneous; it may seem like that, even to me, but my subconscious has done lots of undercover work. When I shared with my wife the derivation of the idea, which now had moved from 'tiny

What's Wrong?

house living' to '*RVing for at least a year, quitting my job to travel, teach and help others*', her response was 'What's an RV?'

Oh, boy, I had to start from the very beginning. The lesson here is to take your time and keep your (if any) frustration in check as not everyone is inside your head. Be diligent and explain from your point of view, but also understand their points of view. Only then can you try to achieve some understanding. Just know that especially when the idea is different or very different like this one, you have to expect surprise, doubts and even pushbacks of the 'Why do this?' and 'Are you crazy?' category.

You just need to work through them with the people who matter—and with the ones that don't really matter, just ignore and move forward.

Actual prep & needed time

My wife is also an immigrant, coming a bit over seven years ago from beautiful Colombia. We met by fate online at first, then in person. It was a 'click' from the beginning, and we never stopped since then. Our upbringings, while different, were also similar, two young immigrants looking for better lives and opportunities, leaving behind family and loved ones to take a chance. By default, we were both adventurers, even though I've never described ourselves like that before.

She's also traveled extensively within Colombia during her upbringing, which could make one either love travel or hate travel (as you're all traveled out). As I explained to her the idea of RVing, creating a company that would potentially help out thousands of people and students understand about their finances and how to help start them on the right path of financial responsibility, in addition to the thrill of traveling and touring around the country for at least a year, she seemed excited and confused at the same time.

So, I let her be, to think and decide for herself. Over the next couple of months, I could see her reading stories about RVing, different people doing it and their stories and pictures, and she was definitely warming up. But it took about three months until she also was on board, saying 'Let's do it'.

At this time, I had a 'back of the envelope' idea of how it would work and, of course, how much money we would need to make this happen. Naturally, this is not a cheap idea and it would have to work on the 'worst case scenario' as well, for us to move forward. It was time to plan for it all, but not after getting our minds fully prepared for it.

We had a planned, upcoming trip to Albania and Europe and decided that we would finalize our decision after the trip. I just felt like I wanted to see final signs and let our minds really embrace the idea before jumping all in. So, we did; we traveled to Albania, met my grandma and other relatives, and enjoyed time in my birth town as well as the beautiful towns of the Adriatic and Ionion coasts. We then traveled to Italy for few days in Rome and Milan before taking the train to Paris.

All in all, it was a very memorable experience, too much to get in and feel in a short period of time, just two weeks for all that. But I felt like this short trip really gave us the time to see and experience wandering and traveling with purpose. It was our last trip before the big one. There, under the Eiffel Tower we decided that the RV trip was a go, that overthinking it or thinking about 'what could go wrong' would just set us back or make us cancel it. So, now we moved forward with purpose.

Now that the trip was a go, we had to start the whole process of getting ready for it. All the questions came to mind at the same time, the How, Where and When—but in such cases, the 'Why?' is always first. The purpose *always* comes first and if you have a good answer to the 'Why?' you'll always figure out the other Ws. We had the 'Why?' and a strong one at that.

Last-minute test

While we've made up our minds—which is the most important part—there are always hurdles that come up in different forms. It never simply goes smoothly, and you should expect it not to go smoothly. So many things are outside of your control and the point is to see how you respond to these 'tests' and to see how strong your passion and determination are, to move forward. For us, there were many little tests, but the memorable one was the one that pushed our departure ten days later than our planned date. After a work trip to South Korea, I returned very sick with the flu and it really held me down for over a week. I'd never felt that sick in over fifteen years, and it happened to be the week of our planned departure? Really?

But even though no one knows for sure, I felt it was the last test of the Universe to show if I was really ready. How would I fare after it and would fear and doubt crawl back in? Or would I just suffer momentarily and brush it off?

Of course, my mind was made, so I suffered for a week and brushed it off. RV living (in cold February, mind you) here we come.

Why RVing?

RVing and all the readings and searches we did, fit with our adventure souls—the unknown, the possibilities and the opportunities. How do you know how something feels without having it experienced before? You don't, you just have to have faith that all will be fine, open yourself to the adventure and opportunity and let yourself be embraced by it. We did lots of research and read lots of other people's blogs and experiences, but it's never the same, is it? Our souls were being primed for adventure and we just couldn't wait any longer.

For me, this was also a way to escape, to get out of the norm and the comfort zone to see from the outside, to change the viewpoint, to view from the top and to think on my own. I wanted this to be done while I slowed down and relaxed, and for thoughts to come to me, unabridged or unaltered by the noise that usually surrounded me.

On top of it all, this was a personal challenge that we could do it, that we could travel and be out there without a particular place, just travel wherever and whenever, and do it just like a kid again. As they say, not all who wander are lost.

I also love driving, pretty much anything with wheels and some without. It's always been a real favorite thing for me, and combined with the challenge of driving something I'd never driven before (a 32-feet-long RV while towing a car behind – all-in fifty, feet in length) would be a double whammy – the thrill of driving, plus a challenge if I could really do it. Just the thought of it now excites me again.

RVing would also give us an opportunity to see different places and explore most of the parts of US we had never even thought of visiting. Montana, Wyoming, Oregon and more states come in mind; ohh, all the places we would go! Who wouldn't take the opportunity to travel across all of the US and see and visit places they had never been before? For us, this was a dream, especially both of us being immigrants. And while I had traveled extensively, at least half or more of the US still stood completely unexplored.

But this wouldn't come without fears, even after the decision was made.

Fears are always still going to be there, lurking in the background, waiting for a chance to bounce and crawl back into you.

Chapter 2

From Fear to Fearless

This is what I wrote on 'Fears' while on our third week of our trip:

What is Fear doing here? Why is this emotion so powerful to make us do things that we would never do without it? How can we make sure that Fear doesn't paralyze us? Why fear in the first place?

While we're on our third week from moving and completely changing our lives by living in an RV, I ask these questions of myself. As fear comes and goes inside me, I want to write about it and see if fear gets weaker or stronger in the process.

Fear seems to be everywhere; Fear is looking for our small mistakes and makes a big deal about each of them. Fear is waiting for our imagination to turn slightly negative so that she can jump it. She's there sleeping, but not really. She's inside waiting for the right moment. So, let's get personal with her.

A couple weeks before we moved into our RV, I had a trip to Asia. On the way back, I got really sick with the flu. Whatever it was, it turned out to be a ghastly flu that held me down with fever, body pain and aches for at least one week. After that, with just a few days of a break, I got sick again. This time, it was with the stomach flu, that held my wife and myself down for three days. Fever, body pain, aches and stomach 'stuff'. Back-to-back sickness before getting ready for the biggest change in our lives makes one doubt just a bit.

Fear saw that as an opportunity, went in and spread seeds of doubt, *what ifs, what abouts,* and *are we really sure?* You get the idea.

Fear was there all along, waiting for a weak body and mind so she could go in and do her manipulating work. She was happy to put a few doubts in my mind when she found us in a weakened state. Fear seemed content, but I wasn't. So, I did what was best, tried to remember all the reasons for doing this, for being out there in the unknown; and after a while, the body got better, the mind was thinking clear and I pushed back.

'No Fear, no, you cannot take over'.

She moved to the little corner where she usually stayed. Crying a bit, she was.

First week RVing and first snowstorm in York, PA

Then the moving day finally came, and Fear was still in the corner, looking down and sad. Yet an opportunity was getting close for her to come back.

I was strong, confident and looking forward. But of course, something had to happen. While we finalized our move and settled in our RV in York, PA, news of a storm with at least 4-6 inches of snow hit our local channel. I looked at Fear and her face lit up again; she had a grin on her face, waiting for my move. And my initial move was not a happy one. The first week in an RV without really knowing how it operated, let alone in a snowstorm?

Fear got even happier when she learned that the day before the storm, I had to pick up our toad, a Fiat 500 we tow behind. The RV alone is thirty-two feet long, so adding the tow bar and the Fiat makes the length of it all almost fifty feet. I had never driven anything like this before, ever. Well, Fear was so happy, she jumped out of her corner ready to take over. But this time, my body was strong and my mind stronger.

We picked up the Fiat and drove it back, and the more I was driving and seeing how it responded, the more confident I got. I just drove without letting fear paralyze me. The snow came and went, and we did just fine. But Fear was still sitting there all the while, on the edge of her seat in her corner, waiting patiently. And she'll be there for all of you when you too decide to do something new and challenging.

Once out of our first 'moment', I realized that as we were making the biggest move of our lives into the unknown, Fear was actually *supposed* to be there.

She is one of the strongest emotions that comes and goes when big life-changing events happen to us. I understood that she had tried to make me feel powerless and had wanted to take over. But, in just the first weeks of moving, with all the snow and more, we never let her stop us. We did things that would have paralyzed us before, but we passed through them and came out on the other side.

And we found that the sun was—and is—always on the other side of the storm. Not to say that there aren't more storms brewing, literally and figuratively, and Fear is still in her corner, yet under control.

As in the movie 'Rocky V' where Rocky is training his protégé and talks about fear, we know it's inside us, but we have to control it and keep it in check.

So, here's Rocky …

> *"No no no no no no, no, your best friend is a guy named Frankie Fear.*
>
> *"You see, fear is a fighter's best friend. You know, but it ain't nothing to be ashamed of. See, fear keeps you sharp, it keeps you awake, you know, it makes you want to survive. You know what I mean? But the thing is, you gotta learn how to control it.*
>
> *"All right? 'Cause fear is like this fire, all right? And it's burning deep inside; now if you control it, Tommy, it's gonna make you hot! But you see, if this thing here controls you… it's going to burn you and everything else around you up. That's right."*

Fears are what keep us in check, what keeps the candle running, but get too much of it and it completely paralyzes us. For many people, these fears are what keeps them in place, not changing anything even though they may not like the results.

A certain complacency, and comfort creeps in and changing becomes too hard. "I have too much to lose now" is usually how most justify it. So, they put up with miserable conditions at work or relationships just because of what they have invested into it. This is known as the 'sunk cost fallacy' and we put too much effort and weight on the past, even though a rational person wouldn't. We are mostly not rational; we are emotional.

The typical breakthrough, while not easy, is to ask yourself the question: If I didn't have any memory of the past, or of what I have put up to be here, would I still be here now? In finance, it would be: 'If I didn't own this stock, would I buy it now?'

If the answer is no, but you're still holding into it, due to the time, effort or money you've put into it, then it's time to do what's right and act with courage, and let go. The cost has already happened—it's sunk cost—and there's nothing you can do that can bring it back. The earlier you move out of such, the faster or easier it may be to do something you really like or be with someone you really want to be with. As many have said way before me, 'The way to conquer your fears is by facing them'.

We faced our fears one by one and realized that having a mission and a purpose helped us much more than we thought.

Fears control most of you

You cannot but just wonder at how much our different fears control all or most of what we do, every day, in all aspects of our lives. We do so many things not because they're right or they're just, but due to fear. We allow this extremely powerful emotion to guide our most important decisions, and I mean that generally as well as in investing, specifically. If we understand that most of the time, fear exists in our heads and isn't real, we will act much more thoughtfully, make decisions based on facts and rational ideas rather than 'fight or flight', instant try-to-feel-good, adrenaline-induced actions.

Don't believe me?

Then let's look at a typical day, between when you wake up and when you go back to sleep. And what do I know about this that makes me such an expert in it? Admittedly, not much other than my personal experience and my suppressing of my own fears over time, and especially during this trip around the US. And if you still don't believe it, just skip ahead to topics I know better and in which I am more qualified to give an opinion.

But ask yourself before you skip: 'Are you doing this due to not wishing to know the truth about your fears?'

STANDUP

***

You wake up in the morning, to find the alarm didn't go off and you're late.

Your heart is racing (in fear) that you don't have much time to do all that you need to. And now there's more traffic than usual. Or, the alarm went off and you woke up as usual, turned the coffee maker and TV on, to find the local news broadcasting about the two killings that happened last night. Sure, it's Baltimore and we have more killings than your average city, but it isn't much different in other major metropolitan areas and I've watched the local channels all over the US on my trip.

Anyway, you get in your car, hopefully on time and you drive away, highway driving, among traffic and people who don't know how to drive, keep distance or change lanes properly; your heart beats faster (fear) as you just got this beautiful new car.

Finally, you make it to work, say hi to the person in the front desk and go to your office/cubicle/wherever you sit, turn your computer on and wait for the emails.

What's on the agenda today? More crap, more meetings that mean nothing and more talk about teamwork. You try to pretend like you're working, as if not, you may lose this comfy job you absolutely hate. Sounds like your day, so far?

If not, good; then you're not the typical office worker, but for many doing this routine, there's data to show that many don't like the jobs they're in, but they just do it for the money, so there's that big fear of losing their income, their comfortable job, even though it makes them miserable. Again, it may not be you—and if so, congrats.

But fears creep up everywhere else too. Do you say what you think, or is that too much and would it possibly offend someone (fear)?

Do you take that leap of faith in your passion or are you too afraid you won't make a living off of it?

Do you pursue that love of your life or are you too afraid you will be rejected and then feel like shit?

Do you take the road untraveled (fear) and do things your way, even though many will think of you as weird or crazy?

Are you genuine, helpful, kind and loving as you feel inside, or are you afraid that you will be taken advantage by others who confuse your kindness for weakness?

Are you afraid that you'll die prematurely, as many feel after major (other people's) accidents, and then change your habits due to that?

Are you afraid that you're not enough of a good mother, father, husband, wife, friend or relative?

Are you so afraid of an unknown future that you try too hard to control things, even though deep inside, you know you can't control them?

Do you fear stock market crashes, recessions, portfolio losses and money losses in general?

Yep, all those fears and more go through our minds all the time, getting us all extremely tired, trying to come up with answers to imaginary fears that most often never materialize. I'm tired of just writing all of those imaginary fears.

Turns TV on, four dead overnight and a major wildfire plus the first freeze of the year (more Fear).

'Your mind is your prison when you focus on your fear.'
~ Tim Fargo

Look fear in the eye

First, you need to realize that most of these fears are just in your head. They really are.

If you don't believe it, try this as an experiment and run it for maybe a few months or even longer. Write down or take notes on your phone, jotting down every time you feel a sense of fear. Be honest about this please. Give the reason for that fear, what makes you feel fearful—such as, is it about driving, or your boss saying something, or what you watched on TV, something in the family, etc.

Keep good records of these, and if you're the typical person, you'll have to write down something several times a day. As mentioned earlier, run this for a few months, maybe three. At the end of the three months, go back and start reading all your little posts and all your fears you had at that time. Now, months later, how many of those actions/things that induced your fear have actually happened? Like really.

Typically, you'll probably be at less than 1% or most often, 0%. You gave yourself heart palpitations on a daily basis, increased your fear hormone cortisol, and made yourself anxious for something that just never happened.

It never did; you just thought that it would. You worried 100% of those times, when in reality it happened close to 0% of the times. The problem here is not just your heart, which is a big problem if you let stress overcome you on a daily basis, but more about all the opportunities that you missed, didn't see or didn't take because you were wrapped up in your comfy fear blanket. You never opened up yourself to something beautiful that was *beyond* your fears.

What is there, beyond your fears?

Bluemercury founder and CEO, Marla Beck, who started the online cosmetics company that was eventually bought by Macy's in 2016 for $210 million, says that her family motto is, *"If it feels terrifying, you should pursue it."*

She continues, *"If you have discomfort when you're trying something new but you're excited about it, that's exactly the right feeling to have. That discomfort means you're going to learn something new."*

So, what's this whole section on fear and why am I talking about it like I'm a psychologist? Because, fear is the sole emotion stronger than anything else—well, maybe only 'Love' has something to say on this—that can control what we do, how we do it and why we do it. If we let fear run our lives, we'll convert into people who are just too afraid to do anything, take any risk at all or live our lives fully.

If we don't address fear, we cannot even talk about anything else past it, our true selves, our purpose, the meaning of life and what we're here on this earth for.

We would have to stop at 'But I'm just too afraid to do it' and leave it at that. But once we understand that fear lives inside of us, that it is internal and not an outside factor, we can learn to control it, tame it and—at times—completely eliminate it.

It is very important to repeat that fear is internal, because to most people, it seems as if it's an outside event, something that's happening outside of you that's causing you fear.

At that point, you also feel helpless that you can't control that outside event or thing.

But fear lives inside of you and is fed by your insecurities, by your society, by norms, by your culture, religion and what's expected of you. Fear has been inside of us since we were hunting or being hunted by large and wild animals, and now that we don't do that anymore, fear has also transformed into identifying other daily events as that animal running after us. But we all can agree that being eaten by a lion is not the same as getting fired or being rejected by a girl or boy, but our bodies still respond in the same fearful manner. I think perspective helps, and I'll bring examples where there's still reason for fear in this world, but maybe not in our daily lives.

Once we overcome our fears or at least learn to control them, we enter another area of our existence, one that maybe we've never been before. Stuff (murder, chaos, politics, bad economics, family and love issues) still happens all the same, but you don't react to it with fear. You expect it, you know it's there and it doesn't faze you.

While this is under control, a new arena also opens up, opportunities you were too afraid to even think about, new people who you were too afraid to open up to, ideas that you wouldn't even consider, travel and challenges that weren't even on your radar, thoughts that are 'out there' and innovative ideas to do things better and help others better themselves. Time seems to slow down, and it seems like you've seen this 'movie' again and you show confidence in yourself and others notice it in you.

All because you learned how to manage your own fears.

And how do I know about this? Well, again, solely through experience and doing things that I feared. It is exactly the way to manage your fears by going ahead and doing the actions that you fear. Of course, there are exceptions, such as if you fear guns, don't put yourself in front of one, but most of the fears are of the nature that they're not that scary anyways. You're afraid of rejection? Go ask that person out.

You fear you can't do something well? Say, public speaking—then go ahead and learn and do more public speaking. You're afraid of losing your job and not getting another one? Go ahead and take a leap of faith, with some planning first, of course.

It's literally as simple as doing the thing that you fear, and you'll see how fear loses its power over you; you get more confident as you see that the 'monster' you feared was just the shadow of a tiny baby. You get even more confident as you chase after different fears and find out that there was nothing to fear but fear itself.

Last, in my opinion, when we say we come from different backgrounds or that we've had different experiences that made us who we are, deep down, the difference lies in the number and types of fears that we've already faced and overcome.

Our experiences or our backgrounds simply are our 'accomplished fears', and the more experiences we have, the more fears we've overcome. A memorable experience for good or bad, or an experience that shapes who you are and guides you in your life is what's found past your fears. The people with unique experiences or people who are interesting that we'd really like to talk to are the ones who have accomplished or done things that really scare or terrify us. If you've had to endure and experience certain things that people fear, then guess what; you don't fear them anymore, and your start is already ahead from someone that hasn't had that experience.

Point here is that we all come from different backgrounds, but the sooner we face our fears, the faster we cross on the other side of them where we can take calculated risks, be more calm, more mindful, be open to opportunities and just be our own selves.

Fearless doesn't mean Fear-None

Now, being fearless doesn't mean being fear-none. There's still some place for fear to play its role of fight or flight. There are instances in this world where fear plays its role of keeping you alive, and you need to listen to those feelings.

In 1997 Albania, fear was running high. After the collapse of the pyramid schemes where most people lost most of their money, anger, hate and violence were directed toward the government. Chaos was brewing and it exploded with the government disbanding overnight. Jails opened up, military depots were looted, and kids were seen carrying AK47s on the street. Fear for our future, if we would even make it, was really high. But that is justifiable fear and as long as it helps you stay alive without paralyzing you, it is helping by getting you prepared.

Fear gets you prepared before you need to act. The fear of violence committed to you or your family gets your mind going and preparing for 'what ifs'. This full chaotic situation of no police force, no military, no government and everyone for themselves, as if out of the Hollywood movies of 'The Purge' or 'Mad Max', didn't continue for longer than one week. But still, even after that first week, the police force was more of a show and the cities were still run by armed gangs parading themselves with drawn-out AK47s in convertible cars in the center of the city, passing by the traffic police officer who always happened to look in the other direction when they passed by.

When you see that, you know that you need to take care of yourself and prepare, and fear is there guiding you. Many neighborhoods organized and 'locked' and patrolled their entrances to their neighborhoods. Many others depended on each other arming themselves and time after time, shooting in the air just to show that they were armed as well. We had to sleep on the ground just so to avoid any accidental bullet being shot in the air constantly. But in a weird way, hearing our neighbors shooting gave us a warm feeling that we were protected somehow. Warm feelings for the moment, but one that I hope we never, ever experience in our lives again.

Fear keeps your humility in check and is also there to do the same for your ego. Want to show off? The risk of dying while doing that reckless thing is accompanied by Fear, and it's there to pull you back and make you think again, bringing you to the reality that you may be losing your life. If you want to drive at 120 mph while cutting in traffic and not wearing your seatbelt, that is not fearless, that is reckless—and hopefully, fear is there to give you a needed kick for you to slow down, to make you think and check your ego. Is this really worth it? Recklessness is not fearless.

When we talk about becoming fearless, we're always talking about taking *calculated risks* where the potential returns are worth it, but recklessness is never worth the risk.

Calculated risk means that you get to live and play another day, that you're ok even with the worst-case scenario, but recklessness doesn't give you that.

Fear is there to keep you humble, to keep you thinking about survival and keep your ego in check, and that is a little bit of fear that you get to keep.

STANDUP

Chapter 3

On a Mission

How we got here

But how did we get here, to take this adventure, to get out of our shells and let the sun hit our backs, to travel all over with a purpose and a mission? Most often, I won't be able to remember how I got here or there. It's not memory loss, even though my wife would say the contrary; it's more that there's a network of things, places and ideas all intertwining and coming up with 'solutions', many bold and unexpected to solve problems that run in my mind. I've been involved in finance, investment advising and financial planning for over fifteen years now, starting from day-trading stocks and options from my bed in my early 20s, up to today's advising people with multimillion-dollar net worth, to people with negative net worth.

I was working at an investment advising company when the stock market had one of the largest crashes since the era of depression in the 1930s. The 2008-2009 time period comprised the years where many people lost (or thought so, I'll explain later) a big chunk of their savings and investments. Now, of course, there are things that we cannot help, like economic and business cycles that convert into stock market drops and crashes.

Those are known as systemic or systematic risks that we cannot do much about.

Just by being in the stock market, there are those risks, but over the long run, economies improve, and the stock market recovers, thus the systemic risks usually are short-lived. The thing is that most people don't know this, as it's not taught in schools or not learned anywhere else, and together with other principles of personal finance and investing basics, these factors serve as major inhibitors for most people accumulating wealth or saving for their futures. In addition, many financial salespeople who make a living trading through commissions or other activities of a customer, combined with financial media that promote daily trading—and which get more views in times of panic vs. good times—make the situation even worse.

Most people who don't know this information and who use their own untrained behavior against their best interests, fall for such trading activity, selling when panicked and buying when greed or higher prices make the news.

As a result, most people following the financial news cycles, the advice of their financial salesmen (incentivized by frequent trades, or high-cost products) or who copy their behavior, flat out either lose money in the stock market or don't make enough for the risk and hassle that they endure. When disillusioned like this, many turn against the whole stock market, blaming all and everything, saying it's a rigged system and 'throwing the baby with the bathwater'. Many either completely distrust investing as a whole and either don't invest at all or save via saving or checking accounts, making mediocre returns that are eaten away by inflation.

'Oh, you're one of them'

Most people, especially after the 2008-2009 crisis, were becoming more and more convinced that the game was rigged, that investing wasn't for them, and that only Wall Street could make money and not them. I can't remember who or where, but once I was told, 'Oh, you're one of them' (meaning Wall Street greedy financiers, I assumed).

That did bother me, even though it had no base to bother me at all, but I later figured that many people couldn't make the differentiation between 'good' and 'bad' financial people. That did upset me even more, because all my life I had either made financial mistakes, from which I learned the most but which only hurt me, or in my career I'd only looked for the best benefit of my clients, such as how to maximize returns and diversify risk, helping people understand better their financial choices and eventually serving as a trusted financial person to the families I was helping.

I had no reason to be hurt at all, knowing that what I was doing was right, but nevertheless, I was hurt and bothered by understanding that a person who said this was invariably lumping all financial professionals into the same bucket. And that person was either going to learn all on his own and do everything himself (not likely) or would emerge to be completely out of the saving/investing scene (more likely) due to not trusting. He would only realize too late that investing properly brought tons of benefits when done right and with a trusted person.

Anyway, after more investigation, I found out that many people had either completely lost trust in financial help or were very close to it. That didn't sit right with me.

Then I went into full research mode about what most people were doing at that time, how finance was entering or exiting their lives and how prepared or not financially most people were; I sought out all kinds of research of where was all of this leading to.

It couldn't have been any more depressing, but I wanted to know.

So, one of the worst ones is the major 'wealth gap' that exists in developed countries, and specifically the US. The top 20% of people own more than 90% of all the wealth, leaving the bottom 80% to split just 10% of the wealth (Federal Survey of Consumer Finances). 45% have saved nothing for retirement (Economic Policy Institute), 63% couldn't handle a minor emergency of $500 (Bankrate.com survey and other similar surveys) and all that led to more than 72% of people having major stress about money (APA, American Psychological Association). This was affecting people in ways far beyond just the financial aspect, entering other parts of their life with major repercussions.

Many intra-marital fights are about money, and more people are delaying getting married, while students are forced to move back home with their parents, teens and 20s no longer move out from the parental home, and fewer kids are being born.

When you're not financially secure, many things change, and those changes create other unexpected changes. It could even be argued that high student debt, preventing the starting of families could pose a future issue for Social Security viability many years down the road. There are many problems that could snowball and create a perfect tsunami in decades to come.

What is being done?

Really, in short, not much is being done. From the saver's point of view, things are as complex as they've ever been. People don't have the education or financial literacy level to understand what to do, where and how. From my trip all over the country, I met and talked to hundreds of people, and very rarely did I meet someone who had the correct information to take action and do it right.

A majority of people cannot save and are stuck on a paycheck-to-paycheck cycle, while many others are following the latest fads or living the lifestyle of someone who makes much more than they do. Of course, there are people who don't make enough money to pay basic bills, but then there are lots of others who hide their wants as 'needs' and spend as if they make double of what they actually bring home.

'Lifestyle creep' is a concept very true to many; your spending increasing as high or even higher than your income's increases, not leaving much to save even after income growth. Financial knowledge and literacy are very primitive in the US, which ranks 14th in the world in a simple financial literacy test. Many consumers are just going with the flow and mainly getting their consolation from the fact that their friends/neighbors or people they know aren't doing much better—and that is a horrible strategy to take with us into the future. But it's done every day, by millions of Americans.

The young people, in general, have it even worse. Many are coming up with crippling student debt, while their incomes are relatively flat, and they also carry other consumer debt way higher than prior generations.

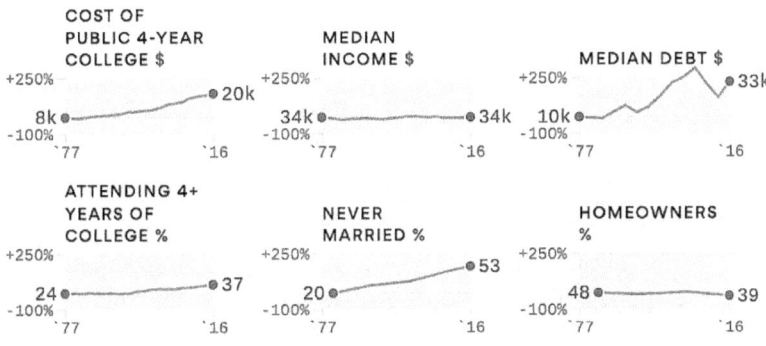

How life has changed for Americans aged 25 to 34
1977 to 2016

Data: College attendance, median income, and home ownership from U.S. Census Bureau; cost of tuition from CollegeBoard; median debt from "The Great American Debt Boom, 1948-2013" by Alina Bartscher, Moritz Kuhn, Moritz Schularick and Ulrike I. Steins; marriage figures from a Pew Research Center analysis of the 1960-2000 decennial censuses and 2010 and 2016 American Community Survey (IPUMS). Note: All dollars are inflation-adjusted to 2016. Chart: Harry Stevens/Axios

Life is different for today's youth – Real median income hasn't changed while debts have tripled.

The financial industry

From the financial industry's point of view, you have the very powerful lobby of the financial services industry who will push hard at any hint of a change from what it is currently being done. Fear tactics abound, from people being scared of losing access to their advisors, to things becoming prohibitively more expensive, to really people not being able to retire if things change—and it's all crap and untrue.

The financial services sector specifically has a big problem with the fiduciary rule, the simple rule that says advisors should do what's best for their client at all times. On the face of it, and if you ask almost anyone if their advisor should do what's best for them or not, then of course, almost unanimously, most people would want an advisor that does what's best for them and has their best interests in mind.

It's a no brainer. But still, the financial services industry will find all kinds of 'experts' to claim otherwise, to claim that sometimes *not* doing what's best for you, the client, is actually what's best for you. What?

It's really crazy to even start peeling their arguments, but again most people are not involved in this, and just hear sound bites of *'your costs will go up if we do this'* and get scared from this really positive change. Big fees, commissions and legal kickbacks are what are holding any of these positive changes from being passed.

Let's talk about 'kickbacks' for starters, and in this instance, legal kickbacks. In the financial industry, there are mainly two types of advisors. One type is a broker, registered to sell financial products and not give advice unless it is 'incidental' and needed to explain the product being sold. The other is a fiduciary advisor. I discuss the main differences in more depth in Chapter 10, but the point is that most people don't know the difference and they're paying heavily for it. The broker model primarily 'hides' the fees from the consumer, as the broker himself is compensated via commissions from the products sold and the customer has to dig deep to find out what he's really paying.

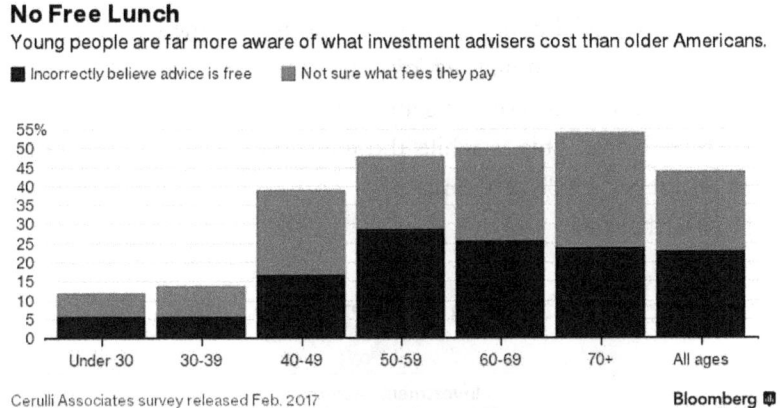

People are not aware of their investment fees

It's no wonder that 20-30% of people think that there are no fees for investing and another 20-30% don't even know what their fees are. And I'd bet the remainder doesn't know all-in fees either.

Cut $5 latte, but pay thousands in fees

Think about it; we know and at times 'negotiate or cut' tiny fees, such as what we pay for cable, subscriptions or different daily items. But we don't know (and many are not so curious to know) what they pay for their investments. Hundreds of articles talk about ditching the $5 coffee, when the thousands or more in fees go unnoticed.

The truth is that during their lifetimes, people are paying thousands or hundreds of thousands in unnecessary fees primarily because they don't know. And when people don't ask or don't know how to ask about how everything works or what it costs, you can hide tons of fees, moving money slowly from the consumer to the financial company. And that's a shame. A good example provided by John Bogle, the founder of Vanguard – one of the most honest and inexpensive financial companies in the industry – mentioned that if a product charges 2% annual fee, over the next fifty years, the financial industry will make 65% of the gains while the consumer will keep just 35% of the gains. This is while the consumer puts up 100% of his capital and takes 100% of the risk.

How is that fair?

Comparing portfolios with different fees

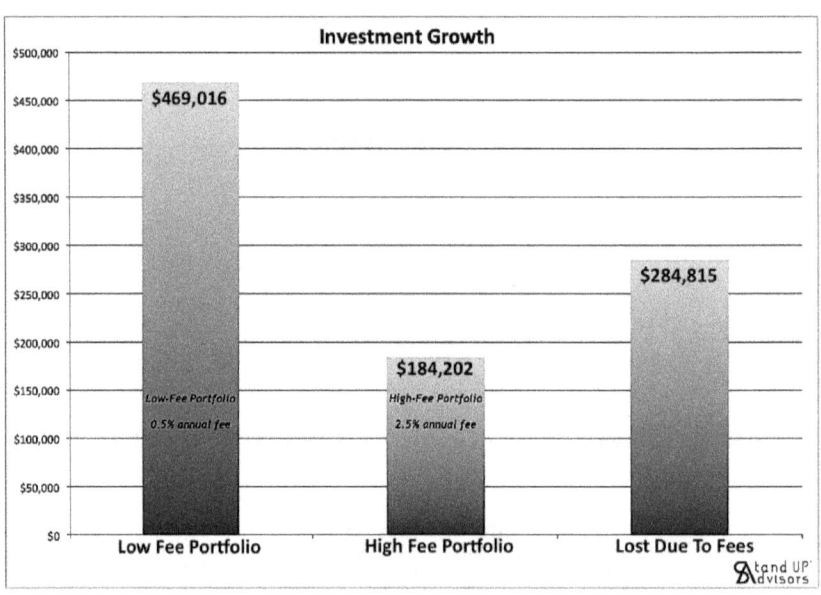

$10,000 invested over 50 years where a 2% fee difference could mean hundreds of thousands of dollars lost due to the high fees (both portfolios earning the same 8.5% annual return)

The second type of an advisor is what's known a fiduciary advisor. They work for Registered Investment Advisory firms and are obligated by law to be a fiduciary and provide advice on the best interest of the client. Full disclosure here; I fall into this type of advisor. So, what do they do that it is different from the broker?

First thing first, as I mentioned above, a broker cannot and should not provide investment advice, so anything that he/she says should be just incidental to the financial product being sold. A Registered Investment Advisor firm, also known as RIA, on the other hand, only provides advice. That means that there are no preferred products because the advice can be provided to go and get any product available, and specifically there are no third-party kickbacks – the advisor is paid directly by the client and no one else, so it is transparent and all fees have to be clearly disclosed. In addition, this closes a major loophole that exists in the broker model, that of a conflict of interest.

When you are a broker and being paid by a third party, especially when you get different compensation from different products, there's always an incentive (and thus a conflict of interest) to suggest the product that pays the broker the most, but when dealing with a fiduciary investment advisor you know that such conflict doesn't exist.

Because there are no third parties paying your advisor for such advice, his loyalty and duty of care falls just on doing what's right for the client. After all, it is the client who's paying the advisor. The alignment of interests, direct payment from the client to the advisor, no other payments except the client's, the transparency of fees, and fiduciary duty enforced by law make such a model much more aligned with clients' interests and really help the client move forward toward their goals.

Conversely, the broker model is not obligated to do what's best for the client. And this is the main problem the financial industry has; if it is obligated to do what's best for the client, that means if it has two products similar in nature and technically doing the same thing for the client, they should offer the lower cost one (doing what's best for the client) instead of the higher cost one. And herein lies the issue — their fees would indeed go down due to doing what's best for the client.

The 'PENTAGON'

Regulators

The other parties to this picture—whom I call the 'PENTAGON' as they're really key to getting things better for consumers—are the regulators, the ones who have to help or look out for the benefit of the consumers using these products and services.

The responsible parties that can make a difference on Financial Literacy

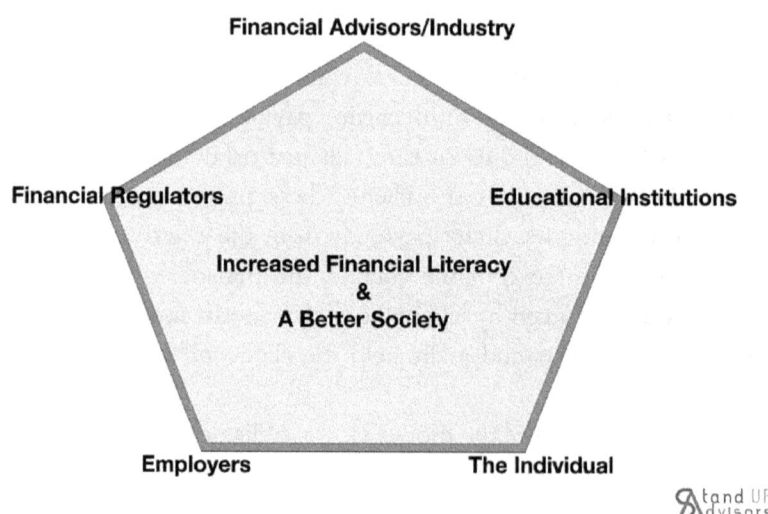

The 'Pentagon' responsible for Increased Financial Literacy

First, you have the SEC (Securities and Exchange Commission) and also the individual states that regulate investment advisors, and then you have the self-regulatory organizations—yes, organizations built by the financial companies to help self-regulate, if that can even work—such as FINRA, that mainly take a role in regulating brokers and their activities. In addition, the Department of Labor (DOL) was also recently involved and pushing for a fiduciary rule for all retirement accounts but was told to stand down by the current administration. In one form or another, all efforts to institute a limited (like the DOL proposal) fiduciary rule or even a more general fiduciary rule by the SEC have failed, spending many years in the 'discussion' phase without any particular rule to enforce and help clients to better prepare for their retirement or other investable goals.

That also tells you all that you need to know, giving you either a complete loss of interest on the topic or a purposeful method to continue doing business as usual. Whatever it is, looking at the sad data for the consumers and where they stand in saving and investing for their future, the regulators as a whole have failed in their duties to help and prepare people for their years ahead.

Educational Institutions

The third group belonging to the PENTAGON are the relevant educational institutions that could help with the basics of financial literacy and educate people to at least understand what it means to save and invest, how to do it properly, how to ask for help and from whom, and how to act with their own best interest in mind.

In my mind, and with information from my Financial Literacy Tour, these institutions can definitely do a lot more. Financial Literacy is rarely discussed in schools and only 40% of states mandate just one such course in their high schools. I believe that colleges need to do even a lot more work, but it has to be done wisely.

For example, when you learn about some basic stuff that doesn't apply to you, like learning the details of a mortgage when you're thirteen, you may learn and maybe retain some, but because the applicability of it is so far away, your mind may not retain enough to remember when it really is needed. That's why I believe that this information is much more important in college or the later years of high school, and what I was proposing to colleges was to hold financial literacy seminars at the right timing when also students would be interested. On my trip, I noticed that while the financial literacy event I held was opened to all college students, the majority of students were either seniors who were ready to graduate or a few juniors with one or two sophomores, and I don't recall any freshmen at all. The point is that they were coming to such an event when it was of relevance to them, a lot more being seniors who were heading into the workforce and who would be faced with such reality of how to budget, where to save, invest and how, rather than others who were further away from that reality.

Education at the wrong time may seem worthless, but if done correctly—and matching it with when students are also interested in the topic—it could be a winnable scenario. While my ratio of interested schools over schools contacted (>1000) was very small, that also has to do with this being an unexpected thing. 'You're from finance and want to help out?' was a common encounter. It may also be linked to the bureaucracy of large institutions and the wish to avoid doing something different or unproven, but I still saw signs of hope. Several schools invited me to speak on this topic; the school contacts knew that this was an important topic that was not being talked about, and one (Scripps College, in California) even started its own program and planned for my seminar to be the opening event for their own financial literacy program. They knew it was really important, and took steps to make a difference, but this can't be said for the majority of schools.

Financial Literacy Event at Scripps College – Claremont, CA

Employers

Employers could also serve a very important role, one that could be of great value to the employees and employers alike, if done properly. If you think about it, you spend more than half your adult time (minus sleeping) at work, and research and observations show that employees are expecting more from employers, not just in terms of a salary, but in terms of benefits and flexibility. In addition to coffee and snack bars or ping-pong tables and lounge chairs, many more employees are asking for benefits that are educational and wellness-oriented, and the 'good' employers are listening and setting themselves apart.

More than 70% of employees mention that money is a main concern they have, either not making enough of it or, very often as I've experienced, not having a good plan for it. While making more money is definitely key, there's a lot that can be done for people who make reasonable amounts but still have difficulty with their finances. Recent research shows that a large percentage of employees bring their money worries to work, lose time at work managing those worries, and drain their attention and focus away from work. One research study by Willis Towers Watson says that financial worries were responsible for 12.4 days a year lost due to 'presenteeism'. This is lost productivity, meaning the employees were at work, but didn't do any work stuff. In addition, there were a further 3.5 days of absenteeism, complete no-shows due to money issues, and not sickness or other reasons. Another piece of research by the Society for Human Resource Management mentions that companies are reporting very low financial literacy of their workforce and that they are seeing such challenges in their day-to-day operations, ultimately affecting their bottom line and profits.

As more companies become aware of this major concern that employees have with money and its proper management, more assistance will undoubtedly be provided by the companies especially when they realize that it will be a great recruiting and retaining tool and an appealing return on their investment. Research also shows that a small investment in financial literacy, education in retirement investing and one-on-one sessions with employees discussing any money matters will go a long way. It shows that the employer actually cares, and it will create a stronger bond with the company, especially knowing that many new employees jump companies every 2-3 years or so.

Many companies have already started programs like this, and I have been a consultant on several. I can tell that employees really appreciate it, and many come with tons of questions, showing up confused by all the financial jargon, and almost all leave satisfied and really happy that they now 'have a plan'. It is a big deal to many, and I've literally seen in their faces a relaxation that only comes from having an objective and a clear path to getting there. The employers offering such services to their employees not only will have much better relations with their employees, but will also improve their reputation, see benefits in recruitment and retention, and will eventually find out that it is also a good business decision. Increasing productivity and reducing time spent on other stuff during work (and money issues is a big one at that) will mean higher profits for the employer while simultaneously increasing employee satisfaction and happiness with their jobs. This creates a usually rare win-win scenario between employees and employers. Employers that realize this win-win scenario will rush into promoting these services and will indeed gain from them, further differentiating themselves in the marketplace of many employers.

The individual

With all those different parties we mentioned, the financial industry, the financial regulators, the educational institutions and colleges and even the employers, not much is being done. The statistics of people's savings and investment accounts show that even if something is working, it is not enough. Of course, you have the top 1% that have million-dollar retirement accounts, paid-off homes and are comfily sitting waiting for their cozy, secure futures, but that's not what I'm talking about. I'm talking about the majority of people, where half of them are not ready at all, with the remainder just poorly or mediocrely ready. But here's a wake-up call: you don't need permission to do something about it. Anyone who is able and capable must come up with different solutions to help in this crisis that expands far from just money and finance alone.

As if you need me to tell you this fact, but just in case it slipped your notice—money is at the center of many other conflicts within families, between partners, and comprises a major contributor to overall stress. In my opinion, this is prime for disruption, for different solutions that can incentivize people to take action to their best benefit.

But this is where it's also the hardest, as people won't take action if it's not a priority or not something that's front and center – and financial future is a far-away concept, only trailing in behind many current pressing issues and worries. For many that can barely cover their current expenses, it's not even a thing, and that's where certain incentives from other parties like employers, schools or regulators and advisors can further help.

Nevertheless, this also mostly requires some personal responsibility, understanding that future financial security is a personal thing and you're doing it for yourself. You have to be ready to think about it internally, and thus the right incentives and financial literacy may work then, but not until you're ready. And that individual is the fifth piece of the Pentagon, which will fall in place when either a person is ready or the other pieces are doing their most to incentivize and promote the individual to take action.

Pursue regardless; the challenge is internal

With all these headwinds and challenges, it would just be very easy to give up, claim defeat in face of so many hurdles and problems that you have to overcome to even make a dent on this iceberg of financial illiteracy. But the thing is that for many people, me included, it is these huge challenges, these completely out-of-favor odds that attract one to do something about it. As with many things, the challenge is always internal.

Do you have the capabilities to do something about it (yes) and then would you do something about it (yes)? Many others do have the capabilities but for very personal reasons, just choose to not stir the pot. So, they leave it as it is and maybe find a spot in the already organized system, as is, even if it really is messed up.

Often, many of those people justify their actions as just not much can be done, or this is always how it's been—and they may even call your attention to 'stop trying to change shit'. But for a few others, it is precisely these out-of-favor odds with a strong desire to do what's right and help another soul that doesn't allow them to 'just let it go'. It is this that makes all the difference and it can apply to any field and any passion that you may have. The challenge is always internal. Will you do what's right and needed or will you just continue making excuses?

STANDUP

Chapter 4

Be Greedy (Not What You're Thinking)

Greed for knowledge

Every time someone mentions 'greedy', it comes out as a really bad word, as something you'd best avoid. 'Don't be too greedy', you hear people say. In finance, people remember the movie 'Wall Street' and its quote 'Greed is good' as a problem with Wall Street and financial companies as a whole. In this context, 'Greed' is always mentioned as a bad thing, where in a limited world, one gets to keep more than one needs, while depriving someone else of the same thing. Yes, agreed, that type of 'Greed' is not good.

But what if you're 'greedy' for knowledge, for experiences, for understanding or for helping others? Does that change the meaning of greed in this context? I believe so. All of the ones mentioned are not only limited, but in our society, more is needed, and being 'greedy' in acquiring them is a good thing and should be encouraged.

Such is the need for knowledge, *real* knowledge, not the fast, superficial skimming of what confirms our already held beliefs. In financial planning and the management of your finances, real knowledge is really lacking. People continue to make mistakes and line the pockets of large financial institutions because they don't know, or because they think they know and they're wrong. I always strive for more knowledge, either through books or through continuous reading of different viewpoints.

Ben Franklin said, *'An investment in knowledge always pays the best interest'* while Socrates said, *'Prefer knowledge to wealth, for the one is transitory, the other perpetual'.*

So, while the typical 'greed' is toward money or possessions, greed for knowledge not only is not bad, but also should be encouraged.

In your pursuance of knowledge, very often you run into the problem of TMI or Too Much Information. So, how to make out what is good info, what is marketing and what is just junk? It is hard, but also not *too* hard if you know where to start and how. For me, my knowledge and experience of financial planning started with my own passion of learning, then getting formally educated on the topic, followed by a lot more passion of learning and knowing more than what school could give me. But here lies a big problem too. We've made information so easy to get hold of, or at least it seems so, that in a sense, everyone thinks they know everything. And if they don't, they just Google it, or ask Siri or Alexa. Sure, technology has helped a lot and made mundane tasks (does anyone remember maps and trying to navigate with them, I mean real maps made of paper?) more efficient and more accessible, and either very low cost or free. Now, a large percentage of people have navigation on their cars even for routes they know or even routes that they drive daily. Well, it helps me with traffic, and I can change routes if something happens. So yes, I do it too, but do we ever think that if everyone does that, and if everyone gets the same recommendation to take that back road as the backup, maybe that back road now becomes the one with the most traffic?

I sometimes play it and continue on same route when I get those recommendations, knowing that other people with their navigation on are getting the same recommendation. Sometimes it works and sometimes it doesn't, but the point here is that we've become more and more dependent on this technology and on this mostly superficial information, that we believe we don't need the experts anymore.

Be Greedy (Not what you're thinking)

Google is the new expert, and if not, we'll just find a blog or influencer that talks about it. Really? That's the information on which you'll be making your most important decisions? Do you know the blogger, the influencer, his/her references, accreditations or education and experience on the topic? Look at it in detail, and it's just Joe Bloggs' opinion, and his opinion is then picked up and regurgitated as 'news' or authority by ten more Joe Bloggs lookalikes. Then there's Josephine Bloggs, and she has a crack at it too. And suddenly, one man's opinion is heralded as the Truth for the whole world on a topic.

Ever look at news site aggregators and look for something really ground-breaking, only to feel let down? That's because every news source is merely copying and spinning articles to make them look as if they wrote them. Really, there may be 50 threads on the same topic from 50 sites across the globe—but they all based their 'hot topics' on the very same pieces—which were not even authoritative to begin with.

It's just information that overloads us and then most of the time, we either do nothing or go with a gut feeling, neither optimal scenarios. It becomes frustrating and crippling trying to seek out the real news from all that pointless, superficial blah.

Too much information is paralyzing and sometimes people spend so much time thinking on minutiae and items that are not even that important, really losing the forest behind the trees.

My recommendation for such a problem is to identify the issue first. What am I trying to identify and find out? Then the next step is to *slow down*. I think this step is one of the most important steps out there, not just for obtaining information but for almost everything nowadays. Try to do some research on who are the people with knowledge on your topic, where are they, have any written books or peer-reviewed papers, or have any well-developed websites, then try and get hold of that book or books, or that paper.

Yep, I'm recommending old-fashioned books or their modern versions of audiobooks. Now take your time on understanding the topic a bit deeper and not just from a blog post or Google search.

Now, I wouldn't do this for something really simple or not important, but for something as important as how to invest your money for the next 30-40 years or how to raise your kids, or how to live free and fully in harmony with the world – something big and important like that is worth knowing at a deeper level from real experts who have proved their expertise.

Lastly on this knowledge topic, try to keep it simple.

You'll hear this time after time and again throughout this book. If I could give just a one-liner to someone, it would be 'Keep it simple'. I totally believe in Da Vinci's saying that *'Simplicity is the ultimate sophistication'*, and we people do complicate things in order to sound smart(er), when in reality the best advice is actually a simple one. It may be hard to follow it, but it nevertheless is a simple one. Create a plan for whatever is important to you and address the main 4-5 things that really matter, as most things in life follow Pareto's law, in saying that 80% of results derive from only 20% of the efforts. Identify what causes those results and focus on those 20% of causes.

Many people input a lot more in effort but because they don't identify those 20% most important things that matter, end up spending a lot more effort and time and still getting much less as a result. Imagine if you could just work one day a week (that's 20% of the week) and get paid 80% of what you get paid now. Would you take that deal? I know many people would definitely take it and find the extra time—four whole days—to do other things to make money, but also do other things with their family or create new things, or just learn and read, share, grow and give. It would be great for business and great for society as a whole. But, again, many don't identify that most important 20% and run around wasting most of the time on tiny things that in the big picture, don't really matter. I once heard these referred to as 'busy fools', and that struck home with me.

When I get to investments and financial planning, I'll show you that this law holds very true and most people can even beat financial professionals if they just do a few things right.

Greed for experiences

You don't need to tell the millennial generation about this. Over and over, they mention that they prefer experiences over things and I totally agree. Experiences create memories, some great ones, some not so great and at times, they create some very memorable experiences that may even shape who you are and what you become.

The RV tour for us was a big experience, one that we'll always remember and talk about. Do you remember that spot or this place, or when this happened or that happened?

Those memories come flooding back to you at unexpected moments and give you a slice of the original feeling you had when it happened to you.

Money buys you stuff, but memories are priceless... Mount Rushmore, SD

It is great and nothing that a piece of property or anything that you can purchase can give to you past its prime, days, months or years after you've purchased it.

I'm greedy for experiences and will continue to challenge myself and our family to get out of our shells and experience different things, different feelings, different emotions. I don't care if anyone has done it before or not; it doesn't matter. What matters is how it makes you feel when you think about it. When we were planning for the RV trip, every time we talked about it and what we would do, I got butterflies in my stomach, an emotion of slight fear mixed with lots of excitement and expectations for the unknown. Even now that I write about them, I can feel the emotions I had when we were planning it. It is known that most emotions are experienced in the pre-execution phase, in the period of waiting for that good thing, but real good experiences continue to give positive emotions while you're doing them, as well as after you've done them.

Now, almost two years after our RV adventure, I still feel awe at what we did and how we did it. Sure, many people do RVing, and a few are young, but this was our experience, our unique one and no one has done it exactly like us, no one. I don't say this for bragging rights, but more to tell everyone that what you create and your experiences are unique to only you. They stay in your memories for life at times, and the great experiences change who you are and what you become for the rest of your life.

It just did that to me. I would never have thought of writing a book, and even now, writing about it is an experience unique to me, with my own spelling mistakes, run-on sentences and parts that don't connect well—hopefully all corrected by my editor—with each other. But it is my experience, my memories and my own unique writing about it.

There's nothing more special than having and making your own experiences away from what everyone else is doing or what society expects you to do. You'll always find more joy being you and making your own history, rather than following along the worn path of others before you. I could be wrong, and I'm totally fine with being wrong, because it works for me and that's the point. You are looking to find joy by being you, not by being who the world wants you to be. That is the ultimate experience of living life on your terms, without regrets, full of love and care for one another.

Greed for helping

This is a big one for me, and this was my main motivation for taking this tour around the country. It is a known fact that you get more satisfaction from doing things for others than by doing them for yourself. It is like it has been designed as a win-win solution.
You help others, so of course you're giving something of value to them—and in return, you also get something of value, much more than what you would have had if you didn't give. It's like $1+1 = 22$ and it amazes me how well it works.

Before getting on our tour, well before on the preparation phase, I was introduced to a little book called 'The Go Giver'. I really liked its premise and bought it in the audio version. I listened to it together with my wife, one small chapter after another, listening to the protagonist doing good deeds and coming up with life lessons.

Long story short; if you help others achieve what they want, you'll also achieve what you want. The point is that the help has to be genuine and not given by virtue of looking for that return of favor, but just doing it to help a soul. The first law of the book is 'The Law of Value' which says that your true worth is determined by how much you give in value than you take in payment. Thus, to really increase your true worth, you need to provide a lot of value compared to your 'fee'. And if your value is really high and your payment really low or even zero, then you're maximizing your true worth.

It is amazing to think that you're increasing your true worth, while at the same time charging absolutely nothing. But even though I am a

Certified Financial Planner, even I recognize that there are many ways to assign value to things; it is not all about money. And so, I believe in it. With my financial literacy tour, I believe I was providing the most valuable principles—the 20% from Pareto's law from above—in personal financial management for the little time I had, typically 1-2 hours of a seminar. But at the same time, I was charging nothing for it. While I didn't get paid for it in money, I was paid in satisfaction that something right was being done, no matter how small, and that a few hundred students now knew the basics of money and knew what to do when out of college. It was a reward that I had changed and hopefully lowered some of the financial stress for these few hundred people who I met along the way.

And that to me is priceless—and I found I was 'paid' in much more than money by looking those people in the eye and seeing how thankful they were for my presence there.

Greed for understanding

Last, I'm greedy for understanding. Understanding people and their points of view, and how much more alike we are than we're not. In times where division and politics have made the world more polarized, there needs to be more balanced people who can connect with all others. Understand that we share this world together and we're responsible for what we do or don't do here, not just to ourselves but to many generations after us.

A while back, my ideas were more strict, less bendable and more confrontational, but I realized that even if right, that is not how we can get the other side to listen and open up to their true self. It takes humility, listening much more than talking, and trying to understand other's point of view. Traveling in the RV, we drove mostly in rural areas. By default, those are the largest parts of the US, and we saw that many once-standing factories or even farms had been reduced to much smaller versions of themselves.

What has happened and why do rural areas now have a high opioid problem? What is happening to the hardworking people who provide our food? In the cities where most people live, we just don't see that and never even ask that question. We just go to our local grocery store and buy what we came for and walk out without thinking about the struggle of that food even getting there. We just don't understand it.

Maybe we don't care to understand it.

This is just an example of many differences that we have, and the more we try to get to know each other, our neighbors and even other areas beyond our 10-20 miles of commute, it will be very beneficial into bridging these divides that have opened up recently. We hide behind our computers and social media and very rarely shake a hand different from ours. Understanding others and creating and having an open mind is key to us getting back on track to working together toward common goals. If we continue to push further apart, we will be positioned in two extremes with no room for compromise while progress is stuck in place.

STANDUP

Chapter 5

How to Get it All?

Help yourself first

We heard before in an airplane said to other people, but now that we have a newborn baby, we're even told very specifically by the flight attendants: 'Please put on your oxygen mask FIRST, then assist the baby'. This seems like an 'Ok, whatever' message, but on the below surface it has so many meanings in life. We'll discuss over and over in this book, that it is not about YOU and how we need to Stand Up for others and do what's right. But you can't standup for others, if you can't standup for yourself. You cannot help others if you need help yourself first. And that's why flight attendants stress over that particular phrase. We need to help ourselves first in order to be in a position to help others. And in our society very few things give you that position as the freedom to have the time and money to pursue those worthwhile passions, dreams and the helping of others. In this chapter and sprinkled in almost all other chapters we'll discuss about Financial Freedom, doing the right things and creating the right mindset that will allow you to achieve your own financial freedom so that you can have the time to help someone else. At the same time that doesn't mean put your oxygen mask and then go to first class have a drink, like we do a lot in this country.

On autopilot

We're now on societal autopilot, wanting to believe it or not. Think how much different you're from the people you hang out with and you'll see you're very much alike. The things we do, what we value, the way we spend our time. We spend 1/3 of our time at work, another 1/3 sleeping and the remaining split between traffic, couple house chores and TV/social media. We would like to think we're different, but we're not. I believe it takes a drastic change outside of your comfort zone or usual happenings to make us realize what we've been doing all along. Getting an RV and going on the road, sleeping in it, traveling outside of our common stuff and areas is something completely outside of one's comfort zone and one to make you realize and see things from a completely different perspective. This is just one way, which we did, but there are definitely different ways to think and see differently. Living in a foreign country for an extended period, volunteering full time, meeting new people you have nothing in common, moving into another area or outside of your common surroundings are some other ways to break that *'same shit, different day'* mindset that many have. In addition, from my experience you'll need some drastic change to see different, incremental change doesn't get you there as the common stuff is just too powerful and overpowers any incremental change, and it's just too easy to get back on the 'same sh*t' routine.

Planning or investing

So, how to put on the 'oxygen mask' for ourselves first? In a society marked by bills to pay, the 'oxygen mask' is obtained when one has the resources to pay for expenses while also having the time to pursue passions and dreams. There are many names for this state of being, from 'Financial Freedom' to 'Financial Independence' to the FIRE acronym—Financial independence, retire early.

These all have in common the pursuit of that status where monthly revenue covers monthly expenses without giving up every waking hour of the day time to obtain that monthly revenue. But we don't have to go to the end of the game. Most people cannot realistically get to that part right away, and it takes time, dedication, and a good job or salary—but in my opinion, what it mainly requires is knowledge and a plan.

You cannot get to a particular point without having a plan for how to get there, but that's exactly what the majority of people do. They want to be and get somewhere but expect it to just happen or they simply go at it piece by piece without any cohesive approach or strategy.

Can't see the forest for the trees

To get anywhere at all in moving toward financial freedom, first we have to step back and pull ourselves away from the 'excessive noise' of everyday life.

Many people are looking for what they say is 'happiness', yet they are doing things almost on a daily basis that are pulling them further away from it. Nobody is doing these things *to* them; they are doing it all for themselves, thus pushing their own chances of success further away while stating they desire the opposite.

There's often too great a focus on little things, what's happening now, the current trends and what social media is up to this particular minute and not on the big picture of what really matters, how to get there, how to think and what to do.

So many people are focused on the 'tiny flowers'—pretty at times, sure—but with fleeting beauty, instead of looking at the whole 'forest' with all that it has to offer and the guidance and ideas that it provides.

This is nothing new, of course. Distraction is a natural human habit, and I am not claiming to be immune to it either. But I have tamed it so that I know it doesn't get in the way of my goals. We should also bear in mind that when we have achieved financial freedom, we can spend all day staring at the pretty flowers if we so choose. But we just can't afford to do too much of it *right now*.

Focus on the big picture first – Mt. Washington, NH

'Focusing on the trees while missing the forest'—or, 'can't see the woods for the trees'—is an old expression, but it carries even more importance now as life seems busier as ever. We're always doing something and have no time to even realize what it is that we're doing and if it is adding any value or happiness to us.

The problem with many is that there's no focus on comprehensive financial planning and a lot of focus on which investment to get right now or what to do about this one particular financial issue they have. People follow hot trends, typically get burned, lose money and get even further behind on the path to achieving what they say they want.

In pursuing 'their form of happiness', many take the short cut that leads them even further behind on the path. I've seen it with clients, potential clients, in just regular conversations with others, and I've heard it from other people. The conversation typically centers on one or two main current financial issues. Either which stock to buy now, which mortgage or credit card to get, which house to look at or what's the latest 'trick' in getting out of student debt. There are two main problems I see here.

One: people focus on just one or two current issues *as they experience them*, and not on the whole personal financial plan that looks at all angles, the ones pressing now and the ones that are not urgent but important, nevertheless. Issue two is that people believe in magic. Financial magic I mean. The financial media is also promoting those 'magical stories' with titles like 'How I paid off $100K student debt in 8 months' or anything bombastic like that. How can anyone not click on it? It's like magic, right?

One day you owe $100K and in less than a year you don't.

Magic, for sure!

Then you read the article and find out that there were two people paying off the loan, as a couple, each with very good paying jobs; plus, they were living on a shoestring budget or with their parents and spending nothing else but on their loan. They had no car costs because they borrowed their parents' cars or, when their parents needed the cars for themselves, their friends came and picked them up. They paid no rent, and nobody asked for contributions toward the household expenses. So, was it magic?

Not a bit; it was just a hyper focus on the loan with nothing else, and they were fortunate enough to have a way to make that hyper-focus possible (like other outside help). The article could just as well have been called, 'I paid off $100K by sponging off everyone else'! I jest but at the same time, it's true. There are so many articles around like this that many people are accustomed to believing in magic nowadays. They even sit down with me as a Certified Financial Planner and technically ask for magic then too, without saying the actual word. When I mention the phrase, 'There's no magic' and that what you thought originally in your conscious self-reasoning was actually the path, everyone that I've talked to has understood. People all know that it takes self-discipline, time and, of course, some understanding and knowledge of the choices they have.

Their stomach gets it

But most people, financially educated or not, get it. They initially just want to believe in magic, because it's the easy way to let them have their cake and eat it too. Having said this, this cohort of people who think in pieces on financial matters is a minority that I believe is doing better than the majority! Why is that? It's simply because the majority of people are not even thinking about personal finance at all. Those who are sitting down with me or someone like me already have a grasp to some degree; they are at least looking for advice and taking proactive action. They are at least considering the mess into which they have got themselves. Most people don't.

Most just trust to luck and wait—for the magic to happen.

The statistics as mentioned before are really sad, with more than two thirds of all people not having a small saving account to cover a small financial emergency, and about half not saving for retirement. More than 70% of people are stressed about money.

If you haven't picked up yet where I'm going, it's that financial planning, a comprehensive view of all your financial needs and goals, for now and the future is the best way to look at your finances. A piece-by-piece approach doesn't really work, and this is chasing the idea only when you need it or when it appears relevant to you.

Financial planning looks at *all* parts of your finances including the 'corners' you haven't even thought about. It covers your budgeting or cash flow, money in and money out of the household, your household balance sheet and net worth, your debt management and your emergency fund, your retirement planning and needs, your investments and your risk tolerance, your different insurances to cover you from different risks, your tax management, estate planning (even if you're not rich) and your education planning like 529 plans, so that your kid doesn't have to take exorbitant loans just to get an education.

That is a lot and scary for many, so that's why many people choose the simple path of least resistance, which is *'I'll worry about it later'*.

Which brings me to my next point.

Yes, finance can be complex, and the financial industry can make it even more complex in many instances. But what if it were simple, explained in real talk terms, and enough info to take action but not too much to get you paralyzed? What if that were possible? Would you be interested then?

Why focus on simplicity?

For much of my adult life, I've had instances of too much complication and too *little* complication. While 'complex' pretends to be more thorough, well thought-out and researched and thus more valuable, more and more I see the benefit of simplicity in many or most things that I do. While in search of my simplicity theory, I ran into the quote I hold dearest to me in all my life interactions. It's from Leonardo Da Vinci and it reads 'Simplicity is the ultimate sophistication'.

These five words, as simple as they sound, have a deep meaning to me, especially if coming from one of the most enlightened minds of all times, Da Vinci. I don't know what he was thinking when he said this, but my interpretation, and the one I just believe in, is that in the process of finding the truth on something, you can overcomplicate it and pretend it's 'complicated'. Think of those 'it's complicated' relationship statuses. Why go there? Keep it simple and say what it is. It really is not complicated, most often, it is very simple. It is one or two issues that you decide to rule on, but it becomes complex when the answer of the 'simple' is one that you don't like. So, in short, if one doesn't like how it sounds in 5-10 words, they use 100 words to confuse you and hide the real answer.

Now, with the same mindset, I shouldn't have complicated the above so much, right? Ok, promise I will follow on my own advice going forward. As such, and coming back to personal finance, I believe that simplicity as well as sophistication can be achieved for everyone and without a lot of effort. As I mentioned earlier, I follow a certain rule known as Pareto's Law, where 80% of the effects come mainly from 20% of the causes. Pareto's law has been tested in many different fields, starting from the time of Pareto, of course. Who was he? Pareto was an Italian economist who in late 1800s discovered that 80% of the land in Italy was owned by 20% of the population. Since then, many iterations and very often truly proven tests have found Pareto's Law, also known as the 80/20 rule, to stand true for many other scenarios. Think of how 80% of your profits come from 20% of your clients, or think of the distribution of income or world GDP in which the richest 20% are controlling 80% of the income or 80% of all assets.

Naturally, this rule is not precise and absolute, but it's a good rough representation of what I'd like to use, which is using 20% of the efforts to get 80% of the results.

Who wouldn't like that? It's like studying only 20% of the material and getting an 80% score, or technically a B. The thing is that you still need to know which 20% to study and which 20% is the important part that gives you 80% of the results. That's what I'll try to do in the next chapters, to give you the condensed version, the 20% that will get you 80% or even more of the results in personal finance without complicating it, as simplicity is the ultimate sophistication. Nobody needs complexity and 'it's complicated.'

It also helps me in explaining things and not keeping them overly long, either for me writing it or for you reading it. I tend to be impatient and I get books either in print or on Audible and read 20-50% of it, then just lose interest or let it go. But what if the book was already 50% the size of a regular book, but with all that you needed to know to get on your path to your own financial freedom as well as on your path of helping and standing up for others?

At one point, I even thought of writing a book where the second half of the book comprised just blank pages, but that's just a waste of paper!

STANDUP

Chapter 6

Planning's at the Core

The data is already there, but we just don't know or like it. There's already so much written about investing and personal finance—books galore. And I'm adding this one to that pile. But the issue is that people nowadays don't read much; they just want bites of info and only when it's applicable to them. Like: *'Don't tell me about stocks or diversification right now, I'm trying to buy a house, don't you see?'*

This super-simplified example is what I mentioned earlier—that most people 'busy' with their daily lives attack financial problems only as they come, and typically only when they become a problem. That means they are reactive, not proactive.

Rarely, or only when your income or assets increase significantly, do you start to think a bit more comprehensively, and even then, it is still piece-by-piece approach mixed with generous doses of procrastination. So, I'll try to give you the 20% of what you need to know about personal finance in just these next few chapters.

It will be fast, succinct and to the point, but it may feel too short or 'is that it?'

And that's the problem simplicity brings, that many people feel anything worthwhile and substantial in life has to be long and complex with some professional magic, but I believe otherwise. I have been immersed in the complex world while making almost all of the mistakes, financial or not, and so I can attest that simple is best. Getting the principles right is much more important than what stock to buy or what loan to choose.

Now let's think about basic planning for all. I believe that basic financial planning and knowledge should be available to all, and so I did create a portfolio of short twenty-minute videos on some fifteen topics that cover all personal finance. In just some short six hours, you'll get to know and understand more than 90% of all people—including some professionals—about money, its uses, mistakes and what to actually do with it.

Those videos can be found on my website, but below will be an abbreviated version of that material, so pull up a chair, make a cup of tea, and listen up.

Why Plan?

First, let's discuss the 'Why?' of financial planning.

Why take this time to do it?

The answer is simple; if you sit down and look at all angles of your financial life, you'll see that having a plan will give you clarity of where you are and where you're going. You can notice that where you currently are may not be where you want to be, and even worse, you may not like where that path leads further, such as taking you down the path of having debt that leads to more debt—that leads to further working at jobs that you don't like. Having a financial plan is very important—either if you can create one on your own, or preferably with a good financial planner who asks the right questions and gets you to think what's important to you, but then gives you ways and paths to get there.

The #1 thing that people say when they go through a comprehensive plan is: "I am relieved". I almost always ask everyone how they're feeling after a planning session, and they almost always say, they feel relieved. A cloud has lifted from above their heads. Now, remember what I said earlier; there is no magic involved, so the unknowns are still there and the cloud hasn't magically left, but the clients know where to get an umbrella.

Now, they 'have a plan', and that makes all the difference in their actions, thinking, and mainly, their feelings.

Financial planning is primarily financial, math and rational thinking, but the results are changed feelings and attitudes toward what you're trying to achieve. But why does it have such an effect? Mainly because you start asking yourself what is really important to you, what your goals are and what you are pursuing in life.

It makes you think about your values and then helps you to put your efforts and resources, money and time, toward accomplishing those goals that match with your values. You're asking yourself the questions, and eventually pursuing what gives you that inner happiness. Now, your money and your work efforts in that job that you hate are working toward that freedom of achieving what you desire, not just stumbling blindly toward an empty and temporary high, like the buying of 'things' usually does to people.

You're making a plan to not leave all these important items to chance, and if you've never made or had a financial plan before, that is very important. You now have a say, some type of control over your financial life and you're not just a 'fireman' chasing the latest fire of your own making. You know and feel that if you do this right, you'll have the time to enjoy things that really matter, family, friends, activities that make you happy. And your brain starts thinking positively about all the opportunities that making a plan will give you if all is executed properly.

People who plan versus those who don't – big differences

	Planners	Non-Planners	All
Average Modern Wealth Index score	68	44	50
Pay bills and still save each month	75%	33%	43%
Have an emergency fund	65%	24%	35%
Have life insurance	62%	39%	45%
Feel financially stable	62%	32%	40%
Never carry a credit card balance and make other loan payments on time, or have no debt	42%	26%	30%
Live paycheck to paycheck	38%	68%	60%

Source: Schwab's 2018 Modern Wealth Index

Schwab's survey on people who plan vs. those who don't shows the big gap that planning or not can make for your financial future

Winging it

Planning is still not a favorite sport for many. From a recent Schwab survey, only 25% of people have some type of plan, either written or in their heads. Also, the survey found discrepancies in thinking, in that only 30% of millennials said they had a plan, but more than 60% believed that they'd become wealthy in their lifetimes. This means that half of them believe they'll become wealthy without making a plan for it, and it will just happen!

I have reason to doubt that will come to fruition for these people, because the survey found major financial differences from the people who planned vs. the ones who didn't. For example, while 75% of people who planned saved monthly, only 33% of people who didn't plan saved monthly. Another one was that 38% of people who planned lived paycheck to paycheck, while almost double—68% of non-planners—said they lived paycheck to paycheck. Lastly, 65% of planners had an emergency fund, while only 24% of non-planners had one. And that's why I am skeptical of such a high percent of people who say they will be wealthy (64% exactly) when we notice such a high percentage of people (75%) have no plan at all and thus fail at the basic financial principles they need to have in order to be wealthy. It's exactly as the surveys that find that 90% of people think themselves above-average drivers. It's just another impossibility as, by definition, average is mid-point—and you can't have 90% above average! But we can have 90% of people believing falsely until their belief comes to a crash with reality.

Driving without a license

But we can't just lay all the blame on the people for not planning. I'm a big proponent of financial literacy and education starting early in middle school, high school and then further reinforced in college, and the US sorely lacks that in our education system.

People can vote, go to war and get a six-digit loan for school, but have no idea of the basics of personal finance. In a country like ours, the US ranks 14th in financial literacy, while we have some of the most advanced financial instruments and products.

It's like driving without passing a driving test or having any knowledge, and someone just told you, 'So, here's the steering wheel, gas and brakes. Now GO'.

What about rules, and how to drive?

Well, you figure it out as you go, after you crash several times. That is exactly the way our financial education is currently operating here. Another issue is that people think they don't need a plan, as they don't have much money. That's another myth that makes people make lots of mistakes and lose lots of money. Anyone making 'some' income needs a plan to utilize that money properly and according to what they value.

Everyone.

Another group of people thinks that it is very expensive to get a financial plan or don't know where to get one. This is also not people's fault. The Wall Street machine has rightly made people so skeptical, so they choose to completely throw away any advice, refuse to get educated and know more on the subject, and in the process continue to make mistakes and waste precious time.

Wall Street indeed has a culture of product selling, self-serving and straight abusing customers, and there are many examples to mention in the last ten years or more, starting from the credit crisis and all the way into product pushing and aggressive cross selling at Wells Fargo. But all they got was a slap on the wrist, a fine that didn't hurt them, and a *'don't do it again, okayyyy'* from the regulators.

The people may not understand all the details, but deep down, they feel the unfairness, and many have just pulled back and raised their own walls toward any 'financial person' that wants to help. There are some good ones, but without the knowledge to differentiate, that's also a major barrier in finding a good advisor or planner that can help you.

In your 20s: easy come, easy go…

So, for most that don't plan (including myself in my early twenties) time goes on without making any compounding use of it; consumption and lifestyle creep are the two dominant themes of your financial life and debt is also invited to the party.

First, he gets to know you at school and then debt comes to you through a credit card, or maybe a car loan. Or, if you're the 'responsible' one, he comes via a mortgage. All without any planning, just some mental accounting, not falling off the wagon and not owing to your brother in law or your dear friend.

Life goes fast. You drink and party in your twenties and one day, you turn thirty… *WOW,* you say, *not much has changed financially.* Yes, you drive a nicer car than when a student, and maybe you have a house, but you don't have any money to show for it, as it comes on one side and it departs on the other side.

Does it describe you?

Nooooo, you're the responsible one, right?

In your 30s: are you feeling responsible yet?

So, now that we're in our thirties and maybe thinking of getting married, maybe buying a bigger home or joining finances, you're thinking how to do such. Where to go now? And how to plan for all this? Well, you can keep reading or just go to your local liquor store and buy yourself your favorite poison. I would prefer you kept reading.

First thing you need to do is sit down, *really* sit down, and think of what is important to you. What would you like out of your life? What experiences do you value the most? Is it spending time with family, or is it a nice neighborhood where you'd like to live, or is it making sure your kids are taken care of, or is it being able to travel and see other cultures or be able to retire early (or at least on time)? Or what is it that makes you tick, or excited to be alive?

Please don't say you live to make and have more money, as this is *not* that moment!

Your values & goals

Think about you and what drives you or excites you, and how you want to be remembered when you're dead. Yes, I just said that now.

If you want to be remembered as a nice and generous person, or as a family man or as the fixer of the family or as the 'go to' person for anything, then think about what goals would make you become that person you just dreamt of. What are those goals?

Write them down, no limits, and we'll prioritize them later. Then think about what kind of life you'd like to live, now, in ten years, in twenty, and when you retire and don't want to work any longer or want to work for fun and not because you have to.

Rank the goals from the most important to you to the least important and assign an amount of money, based on your own rough estimate, that you believe will satisfy that goal as well as the timeframe of when you want that goal accomplished by.

You now got yourself a dream map, what you want, by when and what it will take to get there. Visualize it for three minutes while closing your eyes and repeating the goals either out loud or internally. Open your eyes, and now all your goals will be accomplished right in front of you, just like magic... by the power of thinking out loud what you want. Yeah, right... sure they'll be fulfilled, in the imaginary world, they will.

In reality, it takes planning, effort, prioritization and some sacrifice to achieve them all, but at least you have them written down and—hopefully—somewhere hanging right in front of you, so you can see them when you go to bed as well as when you wake up.

On this exercise, it's very easy to get caught up in the societal autopilot and borrow someone else's values. Don't do that; please be you, ask yourself who you want to be and what you'd like out of life and then respond. Also, most values don't even require money at all, but those are the really expensive ones, like honesty, integrity, love, kindness and alike. They take very long to be established and can disappear in a heartbeat.

Some other values and goals do need money, so we'll plan for those, like a nice home, healthy retirement, education, travel & memories and suchlike.

Always think about goals that align with your values.

Here are some typical goals that most families have, just to get your mind working, and some are also recommended for most/all people.

An *emergency fund*, covering at least 3-6 months of expenses, is recommended for all people.

A *retirement goal*, a *'get out of debt'* goal, a *kids' education* goal, a *'home'* goal, any *'periodic travel, or vacation'* goal and any other custom goal that you may have such as a motorcycle (don't), a new car, a second home, etc.

It would be great if automatically, we could afford them all. Maybe we wouldn't even need to plan, as we could just throw money at all of them. But for most of us, that is just not the case. So, what we need to do is think and prioritize them based on the importance they have for us. Some are even recommended by financial planners like me to make sure you don't forget an important goal, like an emergency fund, before saving and buying your motorcycle (again, don't), for example. After prioritization, then we look for assets or money we already have that could be designated for that goal and filling the first priority goals first while moving down on the others. What very often happens, especially if you're young or starting out, is that there aren't many assets or much money accumulated, and most of it has to come (you guessed it) from budgeting.

You either have the money or are working and making money, or for the tiny few trust fund babies, you'll be getting the money later, but you won't be reading this book anyways, so we won't talk about that. What it comes down to is budgeting.

The money you make periodically can be divided between spending and saving, and that savings slice can be further sliced for your specific saving and investing goals.

STANDUP

Chapter 7

Budgeting, Net Worth & Debt Management

Have you fallen for the *'get rich quick scheme'* yet?

For all of the people who don't have the assets yet, and are not going to inherit any, the only way to fund your goals is through your budgeting. That's it, so stop looking for a get-rich-quick scheme, as there isn't any. Most get-rich-quick schemes are quick riches for the fraudster, not you. People have tried them all; hot stock picks, lottery tickets, casino games, options trading, horse betting and all other 'overnight successes'—and they don't work. Most take all your money and put you into a bigger hole than where you started. So, now that we've put that to rest, seriously put it to rest, let's talk about what works. What works is considered boring, long-term thinking about where your money is going and making a plan for it. Budgeting is what works.

And budgeting can be done in different ways, from the extreme tracking of every $1 item you purchase to a more lenient 'fund your goals fully and then spend the rest', to anything in between. But it is still called budgeting, like the words or not, I don't care. Through budgeting, you get to see where your money goes, your habits, and then face the reality of *'do we like where it is going'* or would you like to make any changes?

It gives you both the knowledge and the potential control of where your money is going. But only a third of people do budget, and so many spend without really knowing where it's going. And yes, many are surprised when all is added up. *"I spend that much on dining out? Wow,'* is not an uncommon phrase I hear. You'd think people would know, but items spent over different periods of time don't add up sometimes in our minds.

We forget, and over the month, those small lunches, happy hours, dinners and beers all accrue into some pretty big spending.

Money in and money out

So, start by looking at your paycheck and add any other (if any) income you may have, any side gig, any dividends or rental income or others. This is the money coming into the household. Looking at the money out of the household, we'd have to spend a bit more time. Try to look through your spending over a 3-6-month period to take an average, as some months could be higher and some lower. Then we can start our evaluation. My system for an easy understanding of your OUT money is to divide it into 3 'buckets'.

The first 'bucket' is to include your necessities, things you have to pay no matter what, like rent or mortgage, debt payments, living expenses like food, transportation, utilities, healthcare, kids' expenses and any insurance payments.

My rule is that this section should total no more than 65% of your total gross income, where the largest item, housing costs, should not surpass 28% of your gross income.

Taxes are also included in this 65% as we start with gross income, and calculations are run off it. Another rule of thumb to see if you have too much debt or home payment is to stay under 36% of gross income for your home plus your debt payments.

By the way, these ratios were used by the banks themselves prior to them completely bending their own rules in order to qualify more people for homes, but I believe that they still stand as true valuation metrics and if higher than those, a household will feel the issue with either saving or making other spending work.

The second bucket and the most important one for financial freedom, is the savings and investing bucket. My rule of thumb here is to have at least 20% of your gross income going into this bucket, of which at least 10% goes toward retirement investing.

Starting out is the hardest part and you may feel overwhelmed at first, but continue nevertheless... Madison, IN

The remaining half could be saved for other long-term goals, such as buying a house, education savings for the kids or even to making extra debt payments, above the minimums. Many people cannot afford to put 20% of gross income into this bucket, but don't be discouraged. See this as the goal to attain in order to start saving and investing toward your bigger goals, and maybe later you could find yourself able to put in even more than 20%. The idea when you're young or just starting, is to understand and get the picture of where you need to be and work toward it, even if at the beginning, you may not be able to be there right away. Starting small is much better than not starting at all.

Compounding of interest also does perform magic even with small amounts of money, if it has a long period of time.

The 3rd bucket comprises the remaining 15% of gross income to be spent on discretionary items, things we can live without, but that we'd like to have and want some now. Here you have the shopping, entertainment, dining out, happy hours, memberships, travel, gifts and alike. In my experience as a financial planner, it is this category that gets most young people in trouble, overspending on smaller items that are repetitive and happen if not daily at least 2-3 times a week.

Don't cut your coffee (or do, really doesn't matter)

Now, many would say, *yes, cut your coffee* or do this or do that.

As a financial planner, I believe those are lifestyle choices where no one but the individual themselves can decide what to do. What I do, as a planner, is provide the big picture rough maximum that one should spend on that category, and the individual himself should decide how to spend that money based on his or her goals, hobbies and aspirations. Money doesn't know where it is spent, so as long as money is not taken from the other buckets and spent, I don't care if you have ten coffees a day. It is your choice.

Climbing Devils Tower in Wyoming is hard, keeping track of your budget shouldn't be. Use software to help you stay on track.

After you do this exercise and detail all your expenses, you'll want to monitor them going forward. There are many ways and even different software to do this nowadays. I still recommend mint.com or similar software to help you keep track of them, instead of keeping them manually or in a homemade Excel template. If that works for you, that is fine, but usually if something is too burdensome, we tend to avoid and forget it, and it just won't happen.

Set reasonable expectations

Before you can keep track of it, you'll need to set an amount for each category within which you'd like to stay; it needs to be within the above parameters, but also one that's reasonable based on your lifestyle. If you put down something that just looks good on paper but is almost impossible for you to realize, then what will happen is that it will just stay on paper and never materialize.

You want to put down a goal of saving and reduced spending that is achievable and—just like we mentioned in saving small but starting—it's the same here too. You'd want to start reducing slowly while knowing where your ultimate goal is. If you use software like mint.com, you'd want to link all the accounts you use so that the transactions can come onto the software. And also at least weekly, you'd want to visit your transactions, re-categorizing them if needed and putting transactions in the right spot.

Only then will software make sense for your goals and keep you on track.

Budgeting seems hard at the beginning and it feels as it is forcing you to do something you don't want to. But once you realize that it is your money, just that you're choosing to put it into different buckets that are still for you, then slowly but surely you'll spend more mindfully with your goals in mind while also saving and investing for your long and short-term goals. When you don't have any assets, this is all where your money and the foundation for your financial freedom will come from.

Learn it, use it, perfect it.

Your net worth

The next important part for your personal finances is to learn about your 'net worth statement'. Just like businesses, we too have and need to know and track our financial net worth. Also known as a 'balance sheet', this balances your assets (what you own) on one side with the liabilities or debts (what you owe) on the other side.

The difference between your assets and your debts is known as your 'net worth'. So, if you liquidated all your assets and paid off all your debts, that is the number that would be left. Don't be discouraged here either, as most often when young and starting out, this number is negative, meaning you have more debts than assets. That is OK. Repeat after me: IT IS OK. As long as we acknowledge it and make a plan for reversing it into positive and then growing it from there, there's nothing wrong with a negative net worth.

It just shows that you have more debts (probably student debt if young and just starting out) and not enough assets.

ASSETS		DEBTS	
CHECKING / SAVINGS	$4,000	CREDIT CARDS	$2,000
HOUSE	$300,000	MORTGAGE	$280,000
CARS	$30,000	CAR LOANS	$27,000
PERSONAL PROPERTY	$10,000	STUDENT LOANS	$30,000
401K / IRA	$40,000	401K LOAN	$0
OTHER INVESTMENTS	$20,000	OTHER LOANS	$5,000
TOTALS	**$404,000**		**$344,000**
NET WORTH	**$60,000**		

Sample Balance Sheet; Assets on one side, debts on another, and the difference between the two to be your Net Worth

We divide assets into three main categories based on their purpose:

1. Cash and savings accounts;
2. Personal use assets (like home, car, furnishings);
3. Investment assets (your 401K, IRA, other investments).

We also divide debts into 3 categories, based on time:

1. Short-term debt like credit card, loans from friends or anything that is typically paid under 1 year;
2. Long-term debt, typically your mortgage, your car and your student loans;
3. Other debt which could include investment loan, 401K loan etc.

The issue with assets and debts is that typically, when we think someone is 'rich', we can only look at the assets that are visible, like the #2 category on the assets above—a nice home, fancy car and maybe nice clothes and furnishings.

The issue here is that this category also happens to have the most debt attached to it. A home may be nice, but it also has a mortgage, and the car can be fancy, but you may not know the car payment the owner pays for. So, we get to see some assets of others, that may entice envy or even greed, without knowing what that person owes on them.

Envy and greed aside, what we should be focused on are instead our own assets, increasing them while decreasing debts.

That is the best way to increase net worth, which is what really matters. Having a $1-million-dollar home, while having a $1 million mortgage on it, is just a show with a $0 net worth if only those two items are considered, and one should really understand investments and doing it right in order to get wealthy.

But I got the big house

Fancy homes or cars are just (mostly) money pits that always ask for more and more without giving much back. Well, it's because they're not investments and just a consumption item, no matter what the friendly realtor or car salesman tells you.

Repeat after me, your own home where you live, is NOT an investment.

It feels like one because typically after many years the price has gone up, but mainly the prices of homes nationwide have just kept up with inflation and not much more.

Also, over the many years, homes need lots of maintenance, time and effort to be maintained and that again is not a feature of an investment. An investment pays you, not the other way around. An investment property, on the other hand, that pays income and has a positive cash flow to an investor, is an investment. As for cars and furnishings, don't even get me started, unless it is your great-great grandma's diamond ring. Yes, that is precious, limited and also an investment. So, in short, your net worth is a very important thing to develop and track since it increases your awareness of what you have and what you owe, how your assets are hopefully growing and your debts decreasing.

It is a snapshot in time, and every time you check it—probably best every six months, so you don't get obsessed by it—your net worth will show you where you stand financially. Awareness and understanding of how stuff works are key, and will make you more aware of the choices you make so that next time, you'll think about it: Will this action increase or decrease my net worth? Hmm, now you're thinking.

The good, the bad, the ugly and the sad

How can we talk about money, budgeting and personal finance without getting to talk about debt, our society's obsession with it and for many the new form of 'hamster wheel'? Our society is obsessed with it; don't have the money, but want it now? Just credit it, that's the solution to most our problems, right? Wrong.

As a country, we carry over $9 trillion in mortgage debt, over $1.2 trillion in auto debt, and over $1 trillion in credit card debt, but the most egregious is the student loan debt at $1.5 trillion, more than tripling in just the last decade as the average student now owes more than $35,000. A total of 45 million people have it, and the total student debt is now the second largest right after mortgages. For many millennials, it's one of their largest monthly payments, and as reports show, it may be deterring them from starting and doing things like prior generations could. But not all debt is bad and coming from a country with no real debt system at all, I can appreciate it's good as well.

So, let's talk briefly about the good, and then jump on the 'expected' bad of debt, and lastly, wrap it with tips and ideas and real ways to get your debt under control and manage it properly—to not just survive, but benefit from debt.

First, I want to talk about the good besides just the money part or the math portion. As mentioned earlier, coming from a country with no established debt system, the only way you could buy something was to save for it fully, wait until all the money was accumulated and purchase the thing you wanted. That may sound OK, or even a remedy for our debt-obsessed society but think about it.

For everything that you wanted, including a house to live in or a car to go to work, you couldn't until you fully saved for it. Also, if you even found someone that could lend you the money, it usually was a relative or friend. Then, even if not mentioned, the loan usually came with the inevitable, 'I did you a favor and you owe me' unspoken message.

I know that people who borrowed this way hurried to pay off the loan even faster than agreed due to this non-financial 'owing feeling' to another person.

Having a loan from a faceless bank takes care of that 'shame' that you didn't have the money and that someone did you a favor. That's the non-financial benefit.

The financial benefits are many as well, if used properly. You get to purchase a home and afford to live in a neighborhood you want without having $300K or more in cash, for one thing. Who can even save that much, unless in your late age?

I also don't believe that a primary home, where you live, is an investment as it's most often promoted by many 'interested' parties like realtors, banks and alike. A home is a place you get to live and enjoy the area, schools, the neighborhood and so on, but don't purchase a home thinking it's the best investment you can make.

A home on average, nationwide, has appreciated by just about 3.7% annually, more or less keeping up with inflation, from many estimates starting since the 1920s.

The most known researcher and now a housing index that carries his name, Professor Robert Shiller of Yale University has conducted a lot of research on the topic and even developed the now known S&P/Case Shiller Index that looks at housing prices in different metropolitan areas. With the exception of some 'good luck' areas like some selected West Coast (think San Francisco, Silicon Valley etc.,) or some selected East Coast regions (think NYC or alike), housing prices haven't done much in the many decades, but just kept up with inflation. In addition, let's not forget all the maintenance costs, upkeep, time consumed, property taxes, insurance and any HOA fees that come with owning, and still—even if a house value has appreciated—the only way to access that money (without getting yourself in more debt again, like a home equity line of credit) is to sell and move and/or downsize somewhere else. Why move you'd say? Because if you wanted to buy a similar home in a similar area then the prices would be similar.

Lastly, we haven't even counted the transaction costs of getting a house, realtor fees, closings costs and such that could add at least 3-8% of purchase price every time you buy or sell, depending if you're the buyer or the seller.

The point being made here is that a home is OK to be purchased with debt but not to be purchased with the mindset of being an investment. It's more of a place you'd like to live and raise your family and other things related to that. In addition, the debt has to be reasonable based on your income and the time period you are planning to live there.

House debt

After getting out of my system that a home you live in is not an investment, let's look at the other points to consider about buying a home with debt.

First is the down-payment, and there are many different programs where you could put down as low as 5% and sometimes even less. But it is recommended to put down at least 20% to avoid an additional monthly cost known as PMI, the private mortgage insurance that insures the lender due to you not putting down 20%.

The next step has to do with affordability and how much to borrow.

The rule here is to calculate all your housing costs, including mortgage, property tax, insurance and any HOA and try to be at or below 28% of your gross income. As an example, if you make $60K a year gross income, your monthly all-in housing costs should not surpass $1400/month ($60K * 28% divided by 12 months).

The issue now is that many banks may themselves approve you for more of a house, but you'd want to follow this rule in order to not fall into the *too much house, and nothing else* trap and regret the purchase later when you can't make all of the payments.

Last, on issues of the house and using debt to purchase it, is that with so many upfront outgoings like closing costs, fees, insurances and very often renovations as soon as you move in, plan to purchase only if you intend to stay and live there at minimum for five years. Many say even longer than that, but I believe that five years is the minimum.

In today's society and with job changing so fast, it's hard to see further than five years, especially if it's your first house.

If prices move in line with the long-term averages and there isn't a major recession during those five years, you'd probably break even in a good case scenario after that time. If you were really lucky and your area, for some reason, appreciated more than average then you could make a small profit, but I wouldn't count on it and would think best case scenario is break-even. If you stay less than five years, it is almost guaranteed that you'll lose money by buying a house, and if you stay longer than five years, your chances of breaking a small profit will improve.

Student debt

The second largest consumer loan out there is the student debt. The Class of 2017 had an average debt each of $37,000 and an average monthly payment of $375/month if wanting to pay it off within the standard ten-year repayment period.

Federal loans have many choices of repayment, and if you're someone with student loans, I would strongly encourage you to get yourself really familiar with those options. There's a federal website full of info on that at studentaid.ed.gov where you can get a lot more info on repayment options and other benefits.

Basically, you have the Standard Repayment option where you repay in ten years, then you have the Graduated Option where your payments start smaller then go higher, but you still get to pay it off in ten years, and you have the Extended Option where you extend your repayment over a longer period, all the way up to twenty-five years.

Last, there are different versions of the Income-Based Option where you can make your monthly payment based on your income.

The Federal Loans—not private loans from a bank or credit company—also have other benefits such as deferment or forbearance that allow you to suspend payments temporarily based on certain eligibility criteria, mainly a hardship or similar.

Lastly, federal loans have benefits if you work for a non-profit or government entity. There, under their Public Service Loan Forgiveness (PSLF) program, you get put into an Income-Based Program, make payments for ten years and after that, any balance still owed on the loans is forgiven. Student debt is a heavy burden for many, but if first taken out responsibly and within some reason and parameters, it still makes sense as a way for many to pursue their education. The debt-ratio rule, stemming from how much housing debt you could afford and what total debt you can handle, says that you should stay within 28% of gross income for housing and under 36% of gross income including all other consumer debt (including housing). So, if someone were to have just a home and student debt—no other consumer debt—then the maximum that one could 'spend' on student debt is 8% (if maxing the housing 28%, and total consumer debt at 36%).

Working those backwards and assuming some averages on typical interest rates for student debt, it means that for student debt to be affordable, your gross income has to be at least 1.5 times your debt. You can run more exact calculations on my website, but roughly, the idea is that if you foresee a salary of $60K out of college, you cannot have a student loan of more than $40K. More than that prevents you from saving for other goals, delays other spending and/or borrowings and may even change your lifestyle going forward.

Budgeting, Net Worth & Debt Management

*Discussing student debt at the Financial Literacy Event
University Of Miami – Miami, FL*

So, first understand what you could be making with your degree, what similar peers are making with it, then calculate what is an affordable amount of debt. Try to be under it and last, if on the repayment side, understand all your rights and options, educate yourself, but also don't obsess about paying it as early as possible to the detriment of not starting saving or investing for your future.

If the student debt is below 5% interest rate, you'd really want to consider investing for the long-term rather than paying extra on your loans. Long-term, disciplined and diversified investing has averaged 9-10% annual on a long-term average basis, so in my opinion it would make sense to start investing as soon as possible and get the longest time to compound your money, rather than paying off early a relatively low interest loan.

Emotionally, we want to pay them off and be debt free, but math says otherwise. The same holds for paying off early a low interest rate mortgage (don't do it), but only do such if you cannot hold yourself responsible for properly investing the extra payments.

Fast cars, faster depreciation

Cars, cars, cars! Ohh, these four-wheeled beauties that make us pay way more than we should for them! Car debt is the third largest consumer debt with more than $1.2 trillion borrowed for them. According to Experian credit bureau, the average loan amount is $30k with the average repayment over $500/month.

You can calculate yourself how much of a car or monthly payment you can afford by using the rule of 36%, adding all your housing costs and any other debts you have and then making sure that adding your car payments still comes out to be under 36% of your gross income. Another rough rule of thumb here is spending no more than 35% of your gross annual income on a car, so for example, if you make $50K, you can afford at most an $18K car. That's it, not a $30K car. Spending more or buying at a higher price than you can afford, even if approved for it, will make us feel cool for a minute, but then it will prevent you from following your dreams and saving and investing for your other goals.

I myself did it and it was cool for a while, but looking back, maybe I could have saved and invested all that money in my 20s. But I didn't know any better and didn't have the guidance you're getting now.

Credit cards for anyone, as long as have a pulse

Last in the consumer debt mountain come the credit cards with slightly over $1 trillion in total in the US. Credit cards are some of the riskiest types of loans. They have some limited benefits such as building up your credit and getting some great rewards based on the cards you use, but those benefits are quickly offset and more if you carry a balance and don't pay it off during the grace period where there is no interest charged.

Credit cards also charge some of the highest interest rates of all credit mentioned above, starting at 15% annual and going all the way to 29% and higher at times. Thus, carrying a balance on them would quickly put you into a vicious circle that is too hard to get out of, as the debt compounds and your partial payments may cover interest only or just a small slice of the principal sum. The best way to use them is only if you could be disciplined enough to not carry a balance and pay off in full at the end of period.

Only then will the benefits like cash back, travel rewards, purchase protections and more become worth the effort. This is also the first loan to pay off as soon as possible, as paying a 15% interest credit card is the equivalent of making a 15% return in the stock market or any investment you can make. Since making 15% returns consistently on the stock market is very hard or almost impossible, if you have such debt, the best and only investment strategy is to pay it off as soon as possible.

If you have more than one credit card, start paying off the highest interest rate card first as that is where you'll save most of the interest, or emotionally you could feel better if you pay off the smallest balance card so that you can retire your cards one by one and give you the perception of progress. This will motivate you even further to getting to credit card balance $0. If you have a good credit score and believe that you could pay off the balances within 1.5 years or so, you can even check balance transfer options (such as on creditcards.com) to see a credit card that offers 0% interest for a period of time.

The longer the better. Transfer your balances there and then pay them off within the 0% period. That will save you even more interest as you pay them off.

Obviously, every strategy mentioned only works if you don't add more credit balances or don't jeopardize your own plan by not paying the balances during the 0% period. In short, credit card debt is not a long-term solution and is best if paid off in full. If you cannot handle it this way, it's best avoided completely until you see credit as your own money that you have to pay off at the end of the month.

Debt in America is a major problem and has trapped many people who either don't understand the above or simply are not taught the above, or who just cannot resist the instant gratification of buying everything in the now. There's also the way the system is built, based on a consumer society. Ads bombard you on TV, then you have the *keeping up with the Joneses or Kardashians* syndrome, and all facilitated by easy credit.

Many people have some form of a consumer credit and as mentioned above, if paying just the bare minimum, the credit will cost much higher than what the original purchase even was. Remember the 28%/36% rule, where all your housing costs (mortgage, taxes, insurance and any HOA) should be no more than 28% of your gross income and including any other consumer debt the total should not surpass 36%.

If you keep your debts under these limits, you'll notice that while you have debt and some low interest rate ones, like mortgage or student debts that you carry for longer periods, it is still affordable and will not cause much stress.

But if those limits are surpassed, then debt will create a constant worry and you'll be added to the more than 72% of people who are worried about money according to the American Psychological Association. At the very least, you need to know and learn credit, as well as understand your credit score and check it for free at either creditkarma.com or once a year at annualcreditreport.com.

We live in a credit economy, and like it or not, you're also a part of it.

Learn it, use it and don't be taken advantage of—but instead, use this knowledge to your advantage and use credit for its benefits, while reducing or totally eliminating its hangover effects. If managed properly, debt can help you toward your financial freedom.

STANDUP

Chapter 8

Retirement Savings

Retirement is one of the largest saving and investing goals for most people, even if they don't know it. It is money that is saved and invested, hopefully prudently, that can be there to support your lifestyle when you are not able or willing to work any longer for an income. Many people think about this later in life when they are faced with their later years, and as such, waste precious early years where even small amounts of money can compound and be significant after many years of being invested.

Still not convinced that retirement savings comprise one of the most important saving goals for you? Ok, sure. Then let's answer some questions.

Will you be able or willing to work forever until the day you die?

Do you think social security will be enough?

Do you even know roughly what it will be when you retire?

Would you want to retire early and then spend your precious time on activities that really excite you and not on others because you have to?

Well, then, all of the answers above can be answered by a sufficient amount of retirement assets that can be attained through proper planning and saving.

And if you still think that you'll just work till you die, as some surveys have shown, think again as you may not even have that choice, one, if your health deteriorates and you cannot work (even if you want to), and second, with the compounding technological revolution, you may find yourself substituted by a 'machine' or AI way before you think you're ready to step down. So, financial freedom is a goal to pursue not just because you want to, but really because you have to.

Retirement savings can be very complex and can be made even more complicated by the financial industry, that, as expressed before, uses this complexity to hide high fees and crappy investment products pitched to a financially uneducated society.

Obviously, not all companies or financial products are like that, but the majority of the big companies and financial products do not have your best interest in mind, no matter what titles and slogans apply. For example, let's take the most recent 'Best Interest' law recently passed by the SEC that doesn't define what 'best interest' is, and technically allows the broker firms to continue to do business just as before, but with more complex disclosures that no one even reads.

Buckets of retirement

So, simply talking, you have three main 'buckets' that you can utilize for your retirement investments. The first one is the 'work sponsored account' such a 401K or 403B that you get to access via your employer. You deposit some money up to the maximums by law ($19.5K in 2020) and the employer may also add as well, known as a match.

After you put money in this 'bucket', then you have to pick investments that are provided, typically a selected list of approved funds. Many firms provide that you could make this contribution either on a pre-tax basis or post-tax basis.

The difference is when you pay taxes on this money, the pre-tax basis means that taxes on this income are not paid when deposited, but paid when withdrawn. Post-tax basis (also known as the ROTH option) allows to pay taxes when contributed, but then have tax-free withdrawals later in retirement.

Sometimes, the above is not even an option for employees as approximately 50% of employers (typically small employers) don't even offer a retirement plan due to costs and complexity. But you have other choices, known as the IRAs (Individual Retirement Account) where as long as you have earned income, you can contribute up to a maximum of $6K per year and even more ($1K more) if fifty years old or older.

The IRAs can also be set up pre-tax or post-tax, based on when you believe it will be most beneficial to pay the lowest taxes on that money. Many also say that $6K is not enough and won't help much, and yes, they may be right to a point. But many people who have 401Ks and also have a much higher limit ($19.5K) don't max their accounts and on average put around $5K-$6K per year on them, according to research from Vanguard.

Saying that $6K is not enough is like saying the ceiling is too low at eight feet, when most people are six feet tall or less. Still, if you have more money to invest after maxing your IRAs there is a third 'bucket' where you can put unlimited amounts of money, and you can designate them for retirement savings as well.

Known as simply a 'taxable account', this third 'bucket' won't give you any tax benefits like the 401K or the IRAs will, but it will provide for flexibility, no limit contributions and withdrawals of money without asking uncle Sam if it's ok to do so.

This third bucket is the last one after maxing all the tax-advantageous accounts such as the 401K, 403B and/or IRAs. You can invest for any goal, not just retirement and you can contribute any amount, at any time you'd like.

So far, we've only discussed in terms of 'buckets' or type of accounts that exist, but we haven't yet discussed what to put inside, which is investments. We'll discuss that later after we discuss the account types and the overall system we have in place for investing.

How to prioritize such accounts?

With these three types of accounts, many ask about which one to do or how to prioritize and optimize their limited amounts of money. *What if I don't have enough to maximize all, what should I do first?* are typical questions.

Without giving personalized advice as every person's situation is different—and that's why you'd want to meet with a qualified financial planner, a fiduciary to look out for your interests and guide you for your specific lifestyle, needs and goals—there are some rules of thumb to follow. First, you'd want to check if your employer is sponsoring a retirement plan, meaning if there's a 401K or similar in which you could participate through your employer. Next question is to check with your employer or human resources personnel and understand your plan, how it works, benefits and most importantly, if there's a company match on the contributions. Typically, most companies that offer a 401K also offer a company match on the range of 3-5% of your salary. The only caveat is that it is a match and you'd have to put your money in first, then your employer will match based on their formula. Here is the opportunity for free money from your employer, but it will only happen if you contribute as well to the maximum, to get the maximum match possible. Any contribution without maximizing the company's match means that you're leaving money on the table.

Maybe you can't reach the maximum at the very beginning and that's OK, as long as you understand that you could get a bigger match if you wanted to. Some employers also offer a ROTH option, meaning that you could put in money on a post-tax basis and get the tax-free benefit at retirement. Typically, this depends on your income and higher income earners tend to get the tax benefit now as they could save on current taxes, more than what they perceive the future tax liabilities will be.

Retirement Savings

It's a total unknown, especially if we're talking about tax rates in thirty years or so, but some estimates could help on making that decision, as well as seeing why it's important to have tax-free money in retirement (ROTH) as they've been already taxed.

Congress can change that too if it desires, but we're talking as things stand now.

After maxing your work retirement accounts to get the maximum match, look at having a ROTH IRA, if no ROTH option exists within the work plan. This way, you are establishing that some future retirement income will not be taxed when withdrawn. ROTH IRAs also have income restrictions, so if you start making more than $124K Adjusted Gross Income or AGI if single, and more than $196K AGI if married (limits as of 2020), you'll slowly be phased out and disallowed to further contribute to the ROTH IRA. Sorry, IRS rules. After that point, you can still max your work retirement account and if that is also maxed, you can put everything else in the taxable accounts where there are no limits.

The idea of optimization is to use the current tax law to get the biggest benefits and fund accounts that have such benefits first, then move into the others that lack such tax benefits. An example of an un-optimized retirement planning is having a taxable account for retirement but not contributing to your work plan while having a match there, as well as not having a ROTH account that in retirement will come out completely tax-free.

In retirement it's best to have all three accounts, as it will provide flexibility to draw money from the account that best serves your needs at the time, while not paying any unnecessary taxes.

How much to invest?

When I have this conversation with clients, typically the question comes, 'Well, how much should I invest for retirement?' And my answer is 'Well, how much are you going to spend in retirement?' The point here is that everything depends on you, what your lifestyle will look like, what spending will you have—some expected and some not, like unexpected healthcare concerns. Where will you live and how much time, money and effort will you put toward accomplishing your goals?

Still, I don't like to say 'it depends', so I'll continue to give you rough rules of thumb so that you'd be able to have an idea of what to do, even though I don't know you or your situation. First things first, give this goal the longest time you have. Sometimes, you have forty years if you're just out of college, and sometimes you have no time to spare and you're almost ready to retire. These two extremes aside, most people will fall somewhere in the middle, but wherever you fall on the age scale, giving this goal the most of your time means starting now. Next is to get learning, in which hopefully reading this book will give you actionable knowledge that you can put to action right away.

So, roughly, if you start in your twenties or even early thirties, you'd want to put 10-15% of your gross income toward your retirement goal. You may not be able to do that right away and say it's impossible now, but just keep in mind where you'd need to be. If you start later, you'd want to save and invest even more than that, and that usually becomes harder. That's why starting earlier is the best advice anyone can give. What money does when it gets married to time is almost magical. And you were hoping for magic earlier, so here it is.

Compound interest

Known as compound interest, it's claimed that Einstein said it was the 8th wonder of the world. Whether he said so or not, it doesn't matter; what matters is that it is a non-linear process, known as exponential growth. And very often, our minds cannot even grasp its power. Let me give you an example.

Retirement Savings

On my RV tour visiting colleges, my title and catch-all of the presentation was: *'Don't waste your 20s; It will cost you $1 Million Dollars'*.

Somewhere toward the end of the presentation, I compared someone that started investing at twenty-two years old after college and with income, investing $400/month until retirement aged sixty-seven, with another who started investing when thirty years old (just 8 years later) and who was also investing the same amount $400/month until retirement.

Sixty-seven is the normal retirement age for someone born after 1960. I assumed a long-term average return for both people. 8% is the annual average, which is reasonable over long periods. The US stock market has a long-term average of around 10%/year over long periods. Linear thinking would look at the time that the first person started investing over the other one and make rough mental calculations. So, the first person invested for forty-five years (67 – 22 years old) and the second person invested for thirty-seven years (67 – 30 years old) and everything else was exactly the same.

What would you expect the difference to be between the two in retirement?

Most people think that the first person would have more money, true that, but how much more, that's the question. Oh, and the $400/month is not outrageous or unachievable and is only about 10% of an average starting salary after college, what's recommended for retirement anyways. Class of 2018 had a $50K/year average starting salary, according to The National Association of Colleges and Employers.

How much more?

Can you guess? If you think that it's only eight years more and that is about 21% more time (45/37 - 1 = 21%), maybe 20-30% more money? Then you think why I'm making such a big deal of it and maybe you double the number in your mind (only after reading this, as I don't think you would have doubled it on your own).

Starting investing in your 20s or 30s - $1M difference

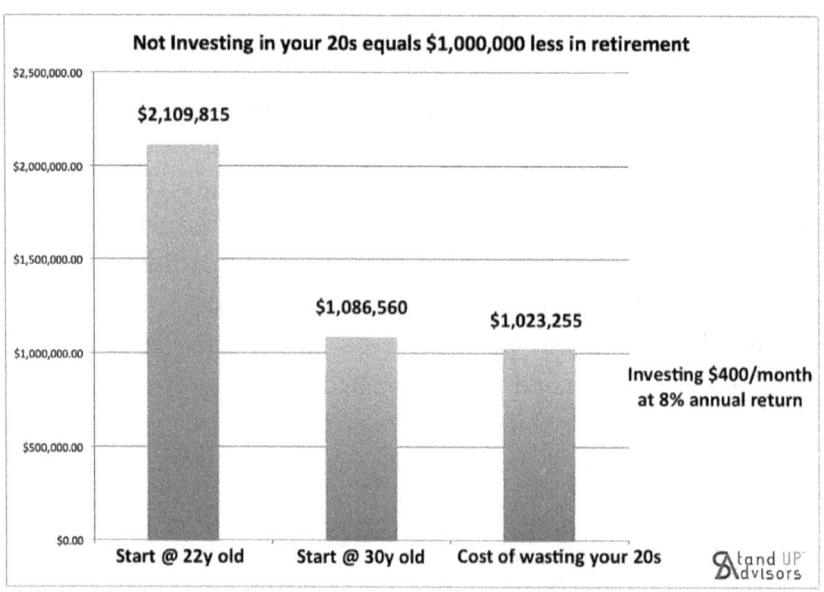

Not investing in your 20s could cost you $1M or more in retirement

So now you think maybe 40-50% more money, right? Maybe, maybe not, I don't know what you're thinking, but good try eh.

Well, suspense over; the first person has almost double the money of the second person (not 20%, not 40% or 50% but over 90% more) and over $1 million dollars more than the second guy. How? Compound interest and exponential growth, which does wonders with time, that's how. The first person would have about $2.1 million in his retirement account (based on my assumptions provided) while the second one would have just $1.1 million, or $1M less. Now, you think back and ask yourself, is waiting those eight years worth a cool $1M?

I don't think that wait is worth it, no matter what you did with that time or money during those first eight years. And that was the eye opener at all the events I had with college students. They could actually do it if they wanted to; they had the time that many don't have and cannot take back after gone.

If this example that shows the power of time and starting early or as soon as possible doesn't convince you, then I am really not sure what example will get you moving.

You're on FIRE

There's a growing movement in US, known as FIRE which stands for Financial Independence, Retire Early, which I'm very familiar with and know people living it, as well as how to achieve it, if that is something you desire.

First, let's get it straight; almost all the young people who aim for or obtain FIRE don't really retire in the sense we think of retirement. They continue to do things, albeit in their own way, starting blogs, podcasts, starting companies, investing in companies and doing things that they care and love. This is all great, and that is why I believe FIRE should stand for Financial Independence, Remain Entrepreneurial.

That second part is a much better description of these young FIRE seekers and achievers. So how to achieve such FIRE at a young age, you ask? It is theoretically simple, but gets harder (or much harder, depending on your situation) in reality.

It's all about income and expenses, and excluding anyone that has inherited money, it's fairly easy to see how it can be possible. This group of people typically has high incomes from working, typically in the six digits, while at the same time keeping their expenses extremely low and saving half or more of their income.

Paired with sound investment strategies which we'll go over later, what gets them to the FIRE status is the very high savings rate of 50%

or higher of their income that compounds over time and gets them to a point where their investments can produce reasonable income for them to cover their daily expenses.

So, increase your investments to that point that you can take a small portion of those investments while making sure that the money will last for your period which could be 40 or 50 years or longer, depending when you decided to go on FIRE.

So, here are some rules of thumb for you FIRE seekers. Try to have a decent income; it cannot be stressed out how important this is, and as cheesy as this sounds, to make more money is a key component of the FIRE opportunity. Then try to live as if you make half or less of your income. Start to see if you can live with half and if that is no problem, see if you can live with a third of your income; that would make your achievement of FIRE even faster.

How to make FIRE work, if you can/want?

Now, let's pull back a minute, and clarify to all the people reading this and saying, 'Are you crazy? I can't even save 5% of my income and you want me to save 50% or more?'

Yes, or no; that is up to you, but that is the only way to achieve this FIRE thing and that is definitely not for all or even wanted by all. It also is not as simple as portrayed by current people on the FIRE track, and many of them have had high incomes, an opportunity to live well under their means, and maybe some luck.

So, let's continue. While you live as if you don't have any money, it may feel hard at times, but your goal is financial independence and achieving the freedom that only a few can. So yes, it is damned hard to do, but not impossible and easier for some and impossible for some others with lower incomes.

Over a few years of investing like this and saving significantly, you'll notice your investment accounts growing slowly but steadily and then getting to a point where a small percentage of that investment sum (around 3-4%) can cover your annual expenses. At that moment, you have achieved your Financial Independence.

An example would be if your annual expenses are $40K a year and your investment accounts, after saving diligently, reach $1M or higher, then taking 4% of those investments annually would be enough to cover your expenses (4% of $1M equals $40K). This is also known as the 4% rule, which has been tested over and over to be a reasonable withdrawal amount, while your assets are still invested in a balanced allocation of stocks and bonds, and able to provide funding for at least 30 years or more.

If you want to be on the safe side, you could withdraw even less, say 3.5% or so, or you could even fluctuate your withdrawals based on your portfolio performance, withdrawing a bit more when markets are doing well and less when markets are doing poorly, if that is even possible based on your expenses. Roughly, if you save half of your income and maintain the same expenses after achieving FIRE, you could achieve financial independence in fifteen years or so, and if you can get to save even more (say 60% or 70% of your income) you could do it even sooner, maybe in 10-12 years.

Now, there are assumptions in here too, like no major recession or depression happens during those years of accumulation and hopefully no major recession or depression during the first few years of achieving FIRE. To prevent or absorb some of this unknown, saving for a bit longer or running your numbers with a slightly smaller withdrawal rate than 4% is what's recommended, especially if you're really young and would want this money to last for fifty years or so. In summary, as you can see, what's needed is the right education, time to get the money to compound, and high income or a high savings rate, but most importantly—achieving FIRE or just simply saving and investing for your goals, it is your behavior and any changes that you may make to the plan that could make it or break it all.

As we'll discuss later, your behavior is one of the most important parts of investing and achieving your goals.

Social Security

Since we're discussing retirement income and savings, let's briefly discuss the social security income and what to expect of it. First, the Social Security Income Fund— according to their own estimates and if no changes are made—will deplete all its reserves by 2034 and then just pay out what it takes in yearly from paychecks, estimated to cover just 75% of what's promised to each individual.

Current average Social Security payment is just a bit over $1500/month, but it was never designed to cover all your expenses in retirement, which means more and more, we have to depend on our own savings, investments and more, as private corporate pensions are almost gone as well. If you were born after 1960, then your full retirement age is sixty-seven, but you can start taking social security as early as sixty-two years old, but at a discount to full-time payments. If you start at sixty-two years, then you'd be getting just 70% of benefits, and every year you wait, benefits increase about 5% annually until age sixty-seven. If you can wait three more years after your normal retirement age to seventy years old, you will be able to maximize your earnings at 124% of your full benefits (what you'd have got at sixty-seven). Thus if you can and don't need the money, or can pull from other accounts, almost always the best bet is to wait till seventy to take your social security payments.

Currently, very few do that, leaving on the table significant amounts of money.

Financial independence is definitely achievable; for some it can be achieved early and for some maybe cannot ever be achieved, but with the right knowledge and understanding of how to optimize the different accounts, and most importantly how to invest wisely, you too can build your passive income and retirement accounts to work for you when you cannot work. Just remember, as many people confuse this, financial independence doesn't just provide you money, but most importantly it also gives you time to do with it as you please, to enjoy it with loved ones or to help others in need or pursue causes you have passion. It is freedom to pursue your life as you like it, unabridged, unfiltered and unscripted on what's really important to you and no one else.

This next chapter, about investments and how to do investing right, is the most overly focused—wrongly in my opinion—section for most people when they talk about money and investing. It's not people's fault either; all the talking heads on Business TV, social media, friends and others all want to talk about investing, about their strategies, how to beat the market, how to trade this fast or go in and out before recessions, come back at the lows etc. and, in my humble opinion, is all BS. So much focus, effort and money are wasted and lost in this exercise that I don't have any silly analogy to bring, but I'd like to switch the focus of that energy somewhere else more important.

I'd still be giving you all that you need to know about investing, tested ideas and strategies that you can use to beat almost any amateur investor and about 90-95% of all professional investors and managers, while doing it simply and not wasting time, energy and funds.

STANDUP

Chapter 9

Investment Strategies & Common Mistakes

I mentioned before in the book that so much effort and time is wasted on investing, and if compared to the overall financial planning, it really is missing the forest for the trees— where investing is the trees and financial planning is the forest.

There's also such an extreme focus on 'beating the market' that it makes you wonder; do you even know 'the market' and why would you even want to beat it? Instead, the focus should be on understating yourself, your goals and passions and your plan for how to get there. The stock market is just a tool to help you get there, if you understand it correctly and don't try to suspend its own laws as many people who try to beat the market attempt to do, unsuccessfully. Investing is about a few principles, some basic rules and mainly discipline and behavior on the investor's part.

I will show you these few but very important rules of investing, as well as some enhancers that have been made available most recently with technology and better advice from real financial advisors, real fiduciaries.

No Free Lunch

But first, what are investments? Very simply, many companies that you know and buy from daily or periodically are public companies and are owned fractionally by the public.

You could be an owner too, if you bought a few shares of those companies. Your shares appreciate (go up in value) or depreciate (go down in value) based on the activities of the company, their sales, management and ultimately their profits, meaning that you as an owner can enjoy either via return of capital—known as dividends—or by further appreciation of the shares. You could be an owner of stock as described above, or an owner of bonds, which technically makes you the lender to these companies.

Stocks and bonds have different characteristics, but mostly what you need to know is that bonds have features that make them less risky, and thus provide less return than stocks, but they provide other benefits as discussed below. As mentioned, 'investments' could vary in risk as well as return, but there is a positive relationship between the two; low risk equates to low expected return, and high risk means high expected return.

If any of these change, like 'low risk – high return' or 'high risk – low return' then you know you have in your hands something that's not right, and it could be either fraud, ignorance on the seller of the product, or even stupidity.

Risk & Return expectations in investing

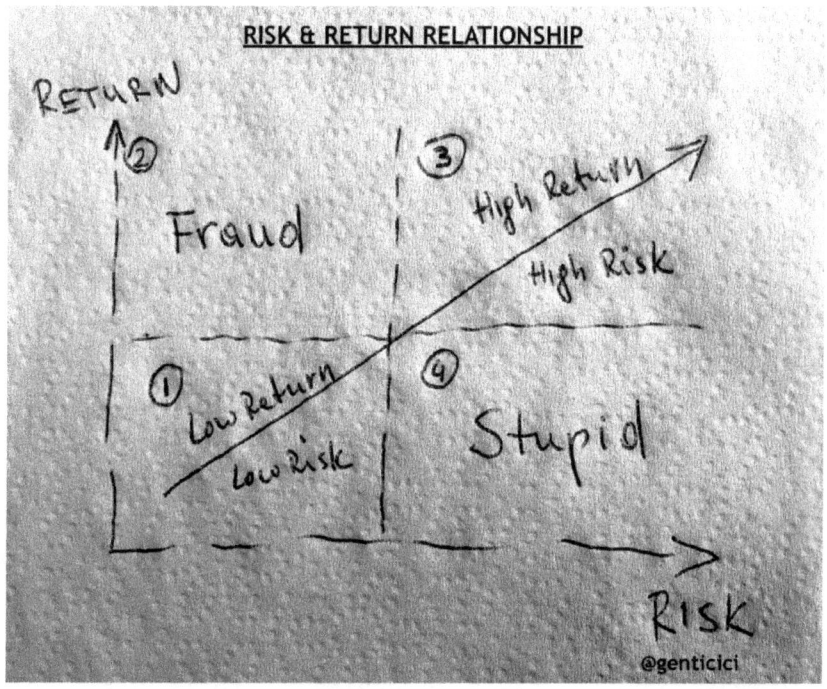

*Understand the risk/return relationship – Beware Fraud and Stupid
Sometimes, I write key concepts on napkins, because the delicate nature of a napkin forces me to keep it simple.*

Remember that if it seems too good to be true, it mostly is, and you cannot have a low-risk product offering a high return, when such a product would be bought up by market participants to bring it in line with the positive relationship that we mentioned, meaning that you wouldn't be able to see it or hear about it at all.

If you still see such product, then look out as you may be the target of something not too nice, to put it nicely. So, there's no 'free lunch' in investing; you get rewarded handsomely—or may lose handsomely—if you take risks and vice versa.

Maybe a 'free appetizer'

The only *free appetizer* in finance is the process and application of what's known as diversification. This is the process of allocating different stocks and funds with varied risk characteristics, reducing overall risk while maintaining or increasing the return.

Simply put, it's finding assets that will zig when others zag, and reduce some of the ups and down of the stock market.

The biggest diversifier and a zag to the zig of stocks are bonds. As said earlier, they have their characteristics that will cushion some of the risks of stocks and almost always—at differing percentages—find their way into a diversified portfolio.

A portfolio is made up of different assets, stocks and bonds mainly, with different characteristics such as the varied geographic locations of companies, different industries and sectors of the economy, that together give an investor a balanced approach to investing wisely. Portfolios could vary from conservative to aggressive based on the make up of the stocks and bonds in them, and they could fluctuate over the short term, with no guarantees on any expected short-term performances. That's despite the fact that over the long run, we could make decent estimates on what to expect.

What's also very important with investing is the compounding effects that are enhanced especially during long period of time. And this is Investing 101 on the 5 minutes it took you to read it, there could be much more, but this is more than most people will even need to know to make good choices with their money.

What really matters?

So, what really matters in investing? There are only a few principles on investing that could make or break your investing plans. Many may want to make you believe there are thousands of variables of how to be successful, and that you'll need their 'secret recipe of success' but the truth is that it is much simpler.

Here are the 6 principles you need to know:

1. Time IN the market, and not *timing the market* is what matters. Many make the mistake of timing, going in and out of the stock market thinking they could go out before stocks go down, and go back in before they move up – which is a big 'good luck' to them from me. Tried by professionals and amateurs alike, this is the worst mistake, the thinking that we know what will happen and by when and how much.

This is predicting the future, and good luck on that, again, especially during these last few years where politics, economics, and global policies are further intertwined, and market movements make even less sense in the short term that they're trying to predict. What matters is *time in* the market, the period you stay and in which let your money compound and grow; that's the big key, and not predicting the future when you have no way of doing so, but only by pure luck. Just a quick example using an 8% average annual return: Investing $400/month for twenty years will yield about $235K while investing the same $400/month for forty years at the same return will yield $1.4 Million. Thinking linearly, you could mistake that double the time (from 20 years to 40 years) then double the return from $235K to, maybe, $470K, but nope. Instead, the return is six times—six, not twice—to $1.4M. Compounding is what makes this possible, while starting earlier so that you have that long-term period to let it do its work.

STANDUP

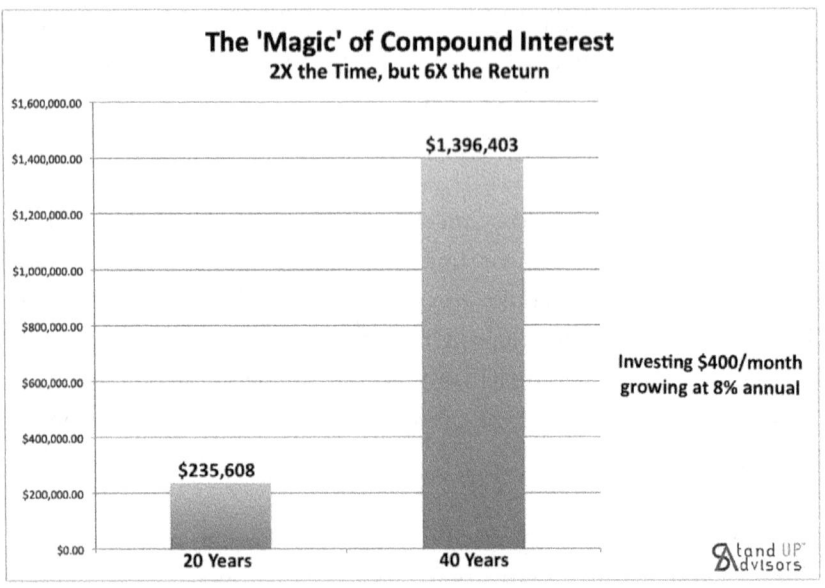

Compound Interest does wonders when paired with time

2. Diversification is the next key concept, comprising spreading your eggs into different baskets and chickens into different pastures, spreading your money into different risk investments, industries and world regions. The world is not just your country, and global diversification allows you to take advantage of growth and prosperity of different countries' economies, even though you don't live there. Most investors in most countries have their money concentrated in just their own country's companies or sectors that they know or like. In some cases, they're excluding 99% of the world economy. If your country's economy is just 1% of the world, why exclude yourself from the 99% of the world's growth?

3. A big factor, that has nothing to do with investments but is an input into them is your savings rate. What you save in order to invest will mean way more than what your investments will return. It is also within your control compared to what the stock market will return,

which lies outside your control. Just a few hundred dollars more a month now, if you start in your thirties, can mean hundreds of thousands of dollars more in retirement. An example, two hundred dollars more or less on a monthly basis may not mean much to you now, but invest that periodically in addition to what you're doing, and it could mean almost $250K more in retirement if you start doing this in your thirties. Your old and tired self will thank you.

4. Investing periodically—and hopefully automatically—has additional benefits as well. You can set up goals, and then investing periodically toward them can make a huge difference, even if you don't have all the money up-front for that goal. It also has behavioral benefits as you just don't have to think about it, and investing is done on autopilot as the market moves up or down. This, known as Dollar Cost Averaging, is another benefit as you'll be buying more shares for the same amount of invested dollars as the market is down; and, as the market improves, which it does over the long-term, your returns will be better as well. An example would be the 'most unfortunate' investor who started investing at the very peak of last market cycle prior to the Great Recession of 2008-2009. Most people fear what will happen if they start investing and then the market goes down. A legitimate fear, but it shouldn't be, for long-term goals with a plan and education. If that investor started investing at the very peak of last market in October 2007 and kept investing monthly (at the S&P 500 index), what would he have? The market (S&P 500) lost over 50% over the next many months, terrifying even the most experienced investors. The recovery, coming back to its high of October 2007, took over 5 years till March of 2013. But this 'unfortunate' investor buying monthly without even thinking had a 38% positive total return for that five-year period. What? Yes, a 38% positive return after the five years that the market recovered, back to when he started. And that was one of the worst crashes, second to only the Great Depression of the 1930s, while other recessions have been quicker to recover. And if you already had money in the market prior to 2007,

that money would have returned to where it was in 2007 (0% returns), but you made 38% on the new money you invested during that period. Let me say it again, 38% return when the market did 0%. But most people panicked, got out and never got back until later, missing on most or all of the recovery.

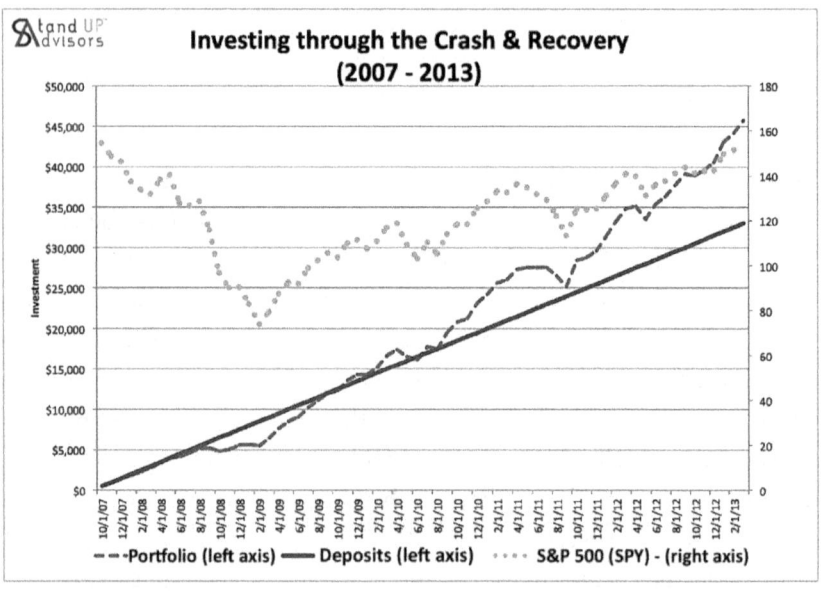

Investing periodically during the last recession as the market returned to where it was prior to crash – (Above example, depositing $500/month for total deposits of $33,000 during the period, investing at S&P 500 ETF (SPY). Investment balance was $45,700 at end of the period for a 38% total return)

5. Another big principle is finding investments and overall investing at low cost. This principle has been proven over and over again to be very important and affects strategies and even the funds' and managers' abilities to supposedly 'beat the market'. It is very important to do the above, be diversified, invest and save as much as possible, but also do it at a low cost. Now, more than ever in the past, this is possible via low-cost index funds, ETFs that mimic the market

and other similar strategies. If you think fees don't matter try to calculate (at my website calculators) even a 1% fee difference on your investments, and you'll see it add up to hundreds of thousands of dollars during your lifetime or much more, and not just due to the fee itself, but also due to lost compounding of the money that went to fees. Many people don't know their fees, but when added up, all the fees very often for small or low balances less than $500k add more than 2%, when you could have a similar or better strategy for even less than 0.1% through a globally diversified ETF (or index funds) portfolio.

6. Lastly, and potentially the most important one, is your behavior and overall discipline with your plan. You could have the best plan in the world, but if it stays just on paper and not executed or if it is changed at the first whim of a 'market talker, talking something bad about the market' then nothing of the above really matters. Your 'good' behavior or avoiding of most of the mistakes that we'll discuss later is what will make most of the difference in the long run. You can properly execute all the principles discussed above and still fail at investing if you make one or two of the behavioral mistakes. It is also the biggest area where an independent, fiduciary advisor can make most of the difference by educating, help in creating the plan, reinforcing the principles and, at times, even 'hand holding' and bringing common sense during times of market turmoil or economic distress. It is those times where most of the advisors truly earn their keep, while educating and calming nerves during tough times where most people are itching to change something in their plan.

Earlier, we mentioned what investments were and what characteristics they had, and mainly discussed stocks and bonds, but there are other asset classes such as real estate, private equity and few other more complex ones that are not really that important for most people. Now, since there are so many choices out there, there's a whole industry of helping people decide what to purchase and also creating products that fit certain criteria so you can invest. The asset management industry, as it's known, is made up of different financial product creators, mutual funds managers, fund companies, index creators, ETF providers and more. No wonder most of this is complex for most people, but let's try to simplify while not losing context.

History of investing

Back in the day, up to mid-1900s, many people were purchasing single stocks and bonds and taking specific risks of the company that they bought. The mutual fund industry, many years in the working, reached its recognition in the 1960s with the premise of fund managers who could pick stocks for you, do all the research, while diversifying into several stocks and reducing single stock risk.

The mutual fund industry grew to giant proportions during all these following decades, as money flew to such managers promising returns of better than just a simple unmanaged index. But first, what is an index? An index is a compilation of certain stocks that fit a certain criterion created by an index company.

So, maybe you have heard the S&P 500 or Dow Jones Industrial Average?

They're both indices that represent a certain segment of the US stocks, based on certain rules put forth by the creator of the index. While an index is not investable, meaning you can't directly buy the index, there are many products created to just follow the index and replicate what the index holds, either as index funds or ETFs (exchange traded funds). I won't get into too much depth of those details but index funds (and index-based ETFs are created to follow an index and do not have any active managers to decide what to buy and/or sell as they just follow the index. As such, they are very low cost, tax efficient and tend to perform better. But more on that later.

So, the big picture in the asset management industry, as discussed above, is that you have active asset management—mutual funds that have managers who want to do better than a simple index—and then you have index funds and ETFs that are 'passive', meaning they're just following the index and not trying to beat it, but just match it after the fees are deducted.

Active vs. Passive

This is known as the *active vs. passive* debate that's been going on in the industry for at least 15+ years. Many have opinions on what's best, but I'll just provide facts and let you think and decide. Active investing is mainly done via mutual funds (or direct stock investing) and those managers try to beat their benchmark or index that they're comparing their strategies to.

Active funds pay fund managers and salespeople, and have other administrative fees, so that's why they tend to be more expensive than passive index-tracking funds.

So, you may say what is the performance? Over the short run, you may see some funds do better than the index, but start looking over the three, five, ten or fifteen-year timeframes and you definitely see the trend of major outperformance of the simple index funds versus the active managed funds. The best record keeper available is the SPIVA Scorecard, produced by S&P Dow Jones Indices, a division of S&P Global, creator of the well-known S&P 500 index.

Active funds compared to their benchmark/index

Report 1: Percentage of U.S. Equity Funds Outperformed by Benchmarks

FUND CATEGORY	COMPARISON INDEX	1-YEAR (%)	3-YEAR (%)	5-YEAR (%)	10-YEAR (%)	15-YEAR (%)
All Domestic Funds	S&P Composite 1500	70.97	69.46	81.66	87.88	87.76
All Large-Cap Funds	S&P 500	69.86	70.74	78.52	88.05	89.83
All Mid-Cap Funds	S&P MidCap 400	35.55	51.41	63.56	85.32	90.33
All Small-Cap Funds	S&P SmallCap 600	35.77	60.59	75.09	87.82	90.25
All Multi-Cap Funds	S&P Composite 1500	72.05	68.42	82.79	89.86	90.15
Large-Cap Growth Funds	S&P 500 Growth	69.49	49.80	65.80	86.47	91.98
Large-Cap Core Funds	S&P 500	70.73	81.29	91.74	96.57	91.81
Large-Cap Value Funds	S&P 500 Value	70.72	67.28	84.74	88.85	79.89
Mid-Cap Growth Funds	S&P MidCap 400 Growth	12.00	20.86	45.45	79.81	86.93
Mid-Cap Core Funds	S&P MidCap 400	43.90	66.94	83.19	91.61	95.15
Mid-Cap Value Funds	S&P MidCap 400 Value	66.04	89.29	92.31	92.98	92.00
Small-Cap Growth Funds	S&P SmallCap 600 Growth	15.25	30.43	59.16	83.77	92.50
Small-Cap Core Funds	S&P SmallCap 600	40.15	76.13	92.27	96.77	93.90
Small-Cap Value Funds	S&P SmallCap 600 Value	60.22	81.98	90.57	97.14	86.84
Multi-Cap Growth Funds	S&P Composite 1500 Growth	54.49	63.18	79.78	90.43	90.44
Multi-Cap Core Funds	S&P Composite 1500	82.17	84.52	96.00	94.26	92.08
Multi-Cap Value Funds	S&P Composite 1500 Value	90.99	72.97	91.35	91.33	85.19
Real Estate Funds	S&P United States REIT	60.00	54.12	66.67	84.78	83.33

Source: S&P Dow Jones Indices LLC. Data as of June 30, 2019. Returns shown are annualized. Past performance is no guarantee of future results. Table is provided for illustrative purposes.

Most of the active funds cannot beat their benchmark/index

The SPIVA Scorecard looks at the performance of thousands of active mutual funds out there, including their fit and category, and compare them with the correct index funds that match their goals and objectives. The results cannot be any clearer.

Over the mid-long run, a five-year time frame on average, more than 88% of active funds cannot beat their benchmark, meaning a simple index fund tracking the index would do much better than almost 90% of all professional managers out there.

The longer the period, the worse it gets for the active funds. Over the ten to fifteen-year period, you can clearly see that 90-95% of all active funds cannot beat the index they're trying to beat. So, there's a very slight chance—the remaining 5% or so—that they can beat the index funds. The issue is that you don't know in advance which will do that, and past performance is definitely not an indication to find that, as many outperforming funds just underperform going forward.

Does performance persist?

Report 2: Performance Persistence of Domestic Equity Funds over Five Consecutive 12-Month Periods

MUTUAL FUND CATEGORY	FUND COUNT AT START (SEPTEMBER 2015)	PERCENTAGE REMAINING IN TOP QUARTILE			
		SEPTEMBER 2016	SEPTEMBER 2017	SEPTEMBER 2018	SEPTEMBER 2019
TOP QUARTILE					
All Domestic Funds	567	17.64	6.53	4.06	0.88
All Large-Cap Funds	220	14.09	6.36	5.00	0.00
All Mid-Cap Funds	80	16.25	1.25	1.25	1.25
All Small-Cap Funds	132	20.45	7.58	3.79	1.52
All Multi-Cap Funds	135	17.04	10.37	6.67	2.22
MUTUAL FUND CATEGORY	FUND COUNT AT START (SEPTEMBER 2015)	PERCENTAGE REMAINING IN TOP HALF			
		SEPTEMBER 2016	SEPTEMBER 2017	SEPTEMBER 2018	SEPTEMBER 2019
TOP HALF					
All Domestic Funds	1135	45.64	24.49	16.83	8.37
All Large-Cap Funds	440	41.82	20.00	15.68	6.36
All Mid-Cap Funds	160	40.62	18.75	15.00	12.50
All Small-Cap Funds	265	44.15	23.02	13.96	7.55
All Multi-Cap Funds	270	43.70	21.85	16.67	8.89

Source: S&P Dow Jones Indices LLC, CRSP. Data as of Sept. 30, 2019. Table is provided for illustrative purposes. Past performance is no guarantee of future results.

Look at how few (or none) of funds stay on the top quartile after being top-quartile funds. <u>There's no persistence in performance.</u>

By understanding this concept of active vs. passive, you not only put yourself in the category of a few, but you also give yourself a peace of mind by knowing that you won't do better by chasing this hot fund or this trendy idea.

It's like getting an A (95%+) without even trying or taking the test, so who wouldn't want that? And lastly, you would be in the 95% percentile of professional managers, but potentially much higher percentile (99%+) if compared to regular investors that make many more mistakes and don't even have the knowledge of professionals.

This big discussion of active vs. passive investing is still ongoing, primarily—in my opinion—due to the heavy fund marketing that the active funds can afford to do, mainly due to their high fees. So, of the high fees people pay, a portion goes into convincing people to invest in the fund even though most often they could do better somewhere else, like in an index fund. As the expression goes, *'It is very hard to understand something if your salary depends on you not understanding it'*.

It's the same here and it will continue, but people have received the message and there have been major money outflows from the active mutual funds into index funds and ETFs in the last ten years or so, and this trend will continue and even accelerate.

What's important to know is that it is very hard to 'beat the market', and most people should focus on what they can really control, such as being diversified and choosing low-cost funds, and primarily watching their own behavior for mistakes that we'll discuss next. It is those emotional hurdles that put most people behind, and not the stock market not performing 'well'.

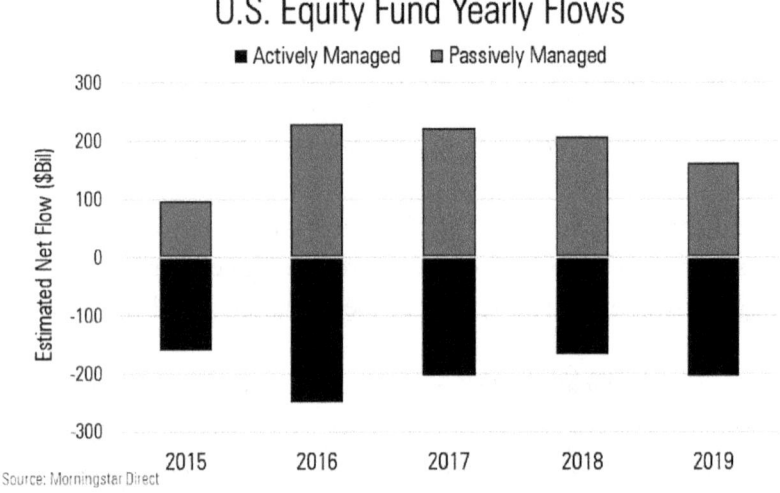

For the last 5 years or so, almost all of the active funds out-flows have been mirrored with the passive funds in-flows

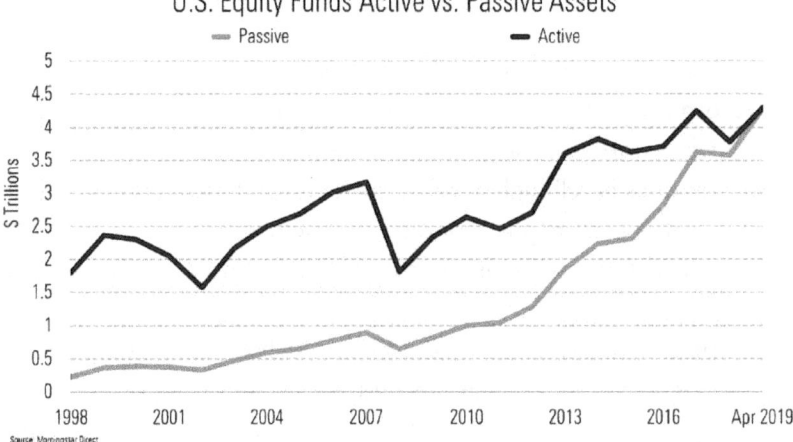

Just a few years back, passive funds had just a portion of the assets of the active funds. But passive funds total assets equaled active funds totals in April 2019, and now on the way to surpassing them in the next few years.

Performance Enhancers

Now, getting the index performance is great and you're definitely in the 95th percentile and higher if compared to your peers, but we can improve even further.

Let's look at some—as I call them—performance enhancers.

There's a lot of research from Vanguard and Betterment and other financial companies, on the use of an independent and real fiduciary advisor. The biggest weight they bring in is the **education, behavioral guidance and coaching** that they can offer, avoiding big mistakes and keeping the clients on an already good path. According to Vanguard, that alone can add up to 1.5% annual to the client's returns. Of course, you don't get to see that as performance on a year-to-year basis, but the idea is that avoiding even one of those big mistakes of selling in a panic, or following fads or funds, or not even investing at all, more than adds up to that if looked at as an annual enhancer.

Another enhancer that could add up to 0.35% annual is what's known as **automatic rebalancing**, where the portfolio is rebalanced—brought to its original allocation—as the market moves up and down. What that does is sell high and buy low, and if done automatically is a process that doesn't require your inputs or emotions.

Tax-loss harvesting is another enhancer now available for all investors.

In the past, that was a reserved feature for high-net-worth investors and required a lot of calculations and trades, and now with the right technology it can just happen in the background as you have your morning coffee. Technically, it's a tax-reducing feature on your investments because taxes really matter, and when done automatically, it is a very good option to add—as Betterment says, up to 0.77% annual returns.

The **asset location** enhancer is another tool to reduce unnecessary taxes and could add up to another 0.75% annual returns according to Vanguard. Lastly, as mentioned before, **using low-cost index funds or ETFs** could add at least 0.5% and up to 2% annual or more if you're currently in very high-cost investments. Put together, all the enhancers used properly with an advisor could add up to 3% annual return or more.

Vanguard called this 'The Advisor's Alpha' or the value that you get by using the right advisor to guide, coach, educate and then utilize the right tools and technology to enhance returns, reduce unnecessary taxes and ultimately help the client to reach his or her goals.

There's a lot to learn from history in life in general as well as in investing. What's been proven over and over in investing is that the 'asset allocation' or where you put or spread your money is what matters, and not the speculation of the day or the trend of the moment. Looking at the long-term trends, you see that the US stock market average tends to fluctuate around the 10% annual. That's looking at the large and known US stocks, such as the S&P 500 index or its equivalent, that the last thirty-year average as well as the last ninety-year average tend to both be around 10% annual. An analysis I came up with, charted below, shows the volatility or price movement that is more visible over shorter periods, such as the three-year period, compared to the longer periods of the ten-year or thirty-year period.

S&P 500 Performance over different time frames

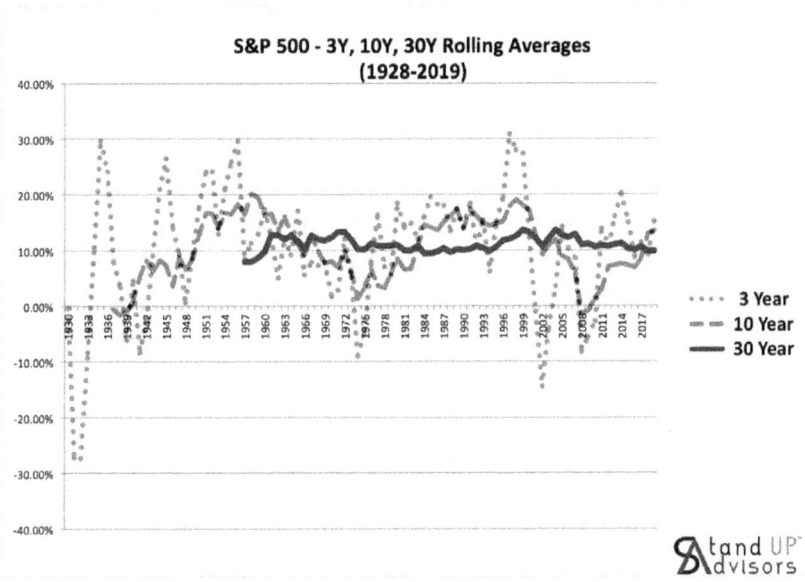

Over the long run investment returns become more predictable

While you can notice several three-year periods where the overall annual returns were negative, you can only see two periods where we've had negative annual returns over a ten-year span, and that was in the 1930s and included the Great Depression, and another with the more recent Great Recession of 2008-2009.

Looking at the thirty-year averages, you see that every thirty-year average is positive and the worst thirty-year average return is 8% annual (from 1928-1957) which includes the Great Depression era.

Let me repeat that; the worst thirty-year performance of US Stocks since 1928, is a very respectable 8% annual average, with the average of all thirty-year rolling periods somewhere in the 10% annual. Of course, and we say it all the time, past performance is no guarantee of future performance, but here we're talking about almost 100 years of history and big-picture trends looking over long periods of time.

I'm not saying we'll never have a thirty-year period that yields less than an 8% annual average, but in the words of Mark Twain, *'History doesn't repeat itself, but it often rhymes',* and I believe that this may well continue, more or less, into the future.

It's not so much a prediction of returns, but more a case of understanding where these long-term returns typically come from, and it's usually from three parts: 1) real growth 2) inflation and 3) dividends that companies pay to their shareholders.

Over these many years since 1928, we've seen high growth, little growth or no growth—or even negative growth. We've seen high inflation or low inflation and we've seen high and low or no dividends at all, and still over the long periods we've come up at these long-term averages. Will they continue? No one knows, but I think that as you lengthen your period of investing, you gain in confidence as the range of returns narrows. Look at the thick line on the chart, and it's almost a flat line compared to the shorter time periods. The stock market gets much 'calmer' and predictable over the long term.

Mistakes, mistakes, mistakes…

The stock market with the returns we mentioned above has the potential to create significant wealth, but very few realize its full potential. According to a company called DALBAR, that's been tracking the individual investor performance for over thirty years now, the individual investor has lagged the market returns by 4-6% on an annual basis over different time frames. The market has returned on average the 10% annual as discussed above, and most investors are losing half or more of those returns due to their own investing style or their own mistakes. Many reasons are mentioned by DALBAR as to why individual investors continuously underperform.

Some mentioned are:
1) the lack of cash to invest (not investing at all);
2) the pulling of cash from investing prematurely due to planned or unplanned needs;
3) high fund expenses;
4) but the largest component of underperformance is and seems to continue to be

the investor's own behavior and emotions that get involved with money and make us act irrationally. Look how an average investor has performed over different periods of time compared to a simple unmanaged index. A huge difference that can be narrowed with the potential help of a good advisor.

Comparing investors' returns with benchmarks/index

	Investor Returns[1]					Bloomberg
	Equity Funds	Asset Allocation Funds	Fixed Income Funds	Inflation	S&P 500	Barclays Aggregate Bond Index
30 Year	3.98	1.85	0.57	2.65	10.16	6.34
20 Year	4.79	2.29	0.48	2.13	7.68	5.29
10 Year	3.64	1.78	0.40	1.83	6.95	4.34
5 Year	9.83	4.85	0.05	1.40	14.66	2.23
3 Year	3.42	1.45	-0.23	1.25	8.87	3.03
12 Months	7.26	5.48	1.23	2.07	11.96	2.65

[1] Returns are for the period ending December 30, 2016. Average equity investor, average bond investor and average asset allocation investor performance results are calculated using data supplied by the Investment Company Institute. Investor returns are represented by the change in total mutual fund assets after excluding sales, redemptions and exchanges. This method of calculation captures realized and unrealized capital gains, dividends, interest, trading costs, sales charges, fees, expenses and any other costs. After calculating investor returns in dollar terms, two percentages are calculated for the period examined: Total investor return rate and annualized investor return rate. Total return rate is determined by calculating the investor return dollars as a percentage of the net of the sales, redemptions and exchanges for each period.

Source: DALBAR

An individual investor has underperformed the index over different time frames

Over the many years in this business, and even prior to doing it professionally, be assured I made a lot of these mistakes myself. I now notice them and see their learning and especially avoiding of them as detrimental to one's management of money and overall finances. The many behavioral mistakes are listed in many behavior finance books so I won't get much in depth on those.

I'll instead describe even more elementary mistakes that many fall prey to, that I myself fell into, and where many people I talk to still fall for one or more of them.

No plan

The big one I usually find with most prospects and my younger self is that many don't have a financial plan and nothing that covers their wants, needs, desires, values, goals and alike in a comprehensive manner. Without a clear plan of what you're trying to achieve, how will you ever achieve it? How will you even know when you have 'arrived'?

Many don't start with a clear plan that outlines their objectives and goals, financial or non-financial, and that's a big mistake. The way I see people address their financial situation is on a case-by-case basis. Like, you need to buy a house, so you find and look at everything house-related but ignore every other part that may relate to it.

Should you even buy a house, would you live in it for five years or longer, or will your payment eat into your other savings goals, such as retirement? As you can see, every financial decision is related to another and another, and they're all inter-related. So, a financial plan is first and foremost and one that many ignore, but they go straight to talking about 'which stock to buy', which is irrelevant and truly unanswerable without knowing more.

Until you sit down to thoroughly think about what's important to you, what you value, how to set up and create meaningful goals for you and then make a plan to achieve those goals, everything else is like choosing a-la-carte vegetables without even picking your main course. You're just fighting the next battle without even knowing what the war is for.

Performance Chasing

The next big mistake by most investors is known as 'performance chasing', where most look at funds to invest for their future by looking at their past performance. While this tends to fall in line with most things we do in life and it's a way we purchase other things, it just doesn't work well in investing. Yes, brands matter in life and give us an expectation of quality—say, when purchasing an expensive car or bag, or any known brand that's typically aligned with higher quality of product. In investing, however, the past performance of a fund manager could very well be down to that manager being lucky or being at the beginning of a trend that will soon disappear.

As we saw earlier, more than 90% of fund managers do not beat their own index over longer periods, so if investing by looking at past performance—and typically people get wowed by great past performance that is significantly higher than the market—it usually means that this performance is temporary and will sooner or later revert.

Every market or trend sooner or later reverts to its long-term average, and that has been true and tested over and over in investing history. There are bull markets that take a certain sector of the economy higher up, more than the regular norm; that is usually followed by a bear market that deflates that trend and brings it back to its longer-term trend or lower.

There are many recent examples like the housing boom and bust of 2008-09, the dotcom boom and bust in the 2000s, the oil boom and busts of the 70s, the precious metals boom and bust of the 70s and, more recently, of 2010-2012. After the bust, most often, prices go even lower than the trend and then with time slowly get back up to their long-term norm.

If you're chasing performance, you'll almost always buy high after the trend shows itself, then may get to ride it higher for a bit, but typically the down wave is almost too soon to enjoy any of the upside. I've made this mistake too, thinking that I could get in and get out before the wave went down, but that's just a dream and I prefer you hear it from me rather than try it yourself. The solution is to match the performance reporting or 'looking' with the goal's time horizon, like if you're saving for your retirement, what does it matter what the market did today or tomorrow? You don't need that money today.

Research by Maya Shaton showed that after the Israeli government prohibited retirement funds from showing performance for periods under twelve months, investors traded less and made fewer mistakes with their investments.

Get rich quick

A mistake that I'll broadly call 'get rich quick' is one that covers many different scenarios, but they all follow the same pattern and mistake.

Very often, when we're not informed about how the markets or investing works, we fall for ideas and schemes that seem too good to be true, which promise fast and high returns with little or no risk. Very often, these schemes fall into the fraud category as if you understood how investing works, you know you cannot have very high returns, much higher than the norms or long-term trends, with little or no risk.

The pyramid schemes in Albania in the mid 1990s fit the criteria precisely, but we didn't have the financial knowledge or literacy back then to understand it. Investing just doesn't work like that. In investing, high return comes by taking high risk and low return by low risk. Any deviation from this means that something is not right, and you should sway away from it. But the 'get rich quick' can also be the legal way, a stock pick that you heard or a rumor of a certain company that is or will be doing great things. You take all your money and buy that stock, effectively putting all your eggs into one basket. Many would look back and say, *ahh only if I put all my money into Amazon or Apple a while back, I would just be a millionaire* and this or that. But again, it doesn't work like that.

You're looking at something after the fact, and now being a predictor of the game after the game is played. How many other companies that did horribly during that period of time could you have picked too? It's impossible to say, but if you think you're good at this, try to pick the next Amazon or Apple. There's definitely one company that will have Amazon's performance in the next ten years if you buy it now, just by laws of probability alone. But do you know which one it is? Are you willing to put all your money in it? I'm not so sure, just like you shouldn't be either. Predicting works best in hindsight but looking forward is a very hard exercise. So, don't concentrate your bets or follow 'get-rich-quick' schemes, as they're typically going to waste your time and money and you'll soon realize that if it is too good to be true, it most often is.

Impatience and getting in & out

A major mistake that typically is combined with the other mistakes above is the impatience we display in investing. We want it to happen in the now, or if not, we bail.

As we saw from the previous charts, during short periods of time, there's a lot of times when performance is not good or even negative; it is only during longer periods of time—10 years+—when the chances of seeing positive returns get in your favor.

But most people hold their investments for fewer than three years, according to many institutions that track these fund flows.

'Nope, this didn't do anything for me, I'll move into something else' is probably a common thought that goes through investors' minds, and that is really a major mistake.

Most don't have a thorough financial plan anyways, so when something happens with the portfolio or the fund or your investment, there's nothing to hold you in it. Having no plan means you can do anything that feels good at the moment, such as selling it, panicking, or being greedy of something else and buying it, further digging into the hole.

Fidelity Investments even did a study on this, on their best performing fund called Magellan Fund that returned on average 29% annual from 1977-1990, managed by the known fund manager, Peter Lynch. Guess what?

The average investor in the fund during that period lost money. You read that right, they lost money due to impatience and moving in and out as performance fluctuated. If you can even find the best investment and still lose money, that shows how important a plan and patience are in investing.

Not using tax-advantaged accounts first

Another mistake that I've noticed is that people don't use the financial accounts in the right order. The different financial accounts available, from 401Ks, to IRAs, 529 plans, HSAs, taxable accounts, and alike are not all created equal, and some have more advantages to be used than others, primarily how they are considered for tax purposes. But also, it matters if they get a company match or not (like many 401Ks). If you're using taxable accounts and investing like that before utilizing your 401K where the employer matches or using a ROTH IRA where you get added tax benefits, then you're leaving benefits on the table.

High or hidden Fees

Last on my mistakes list is 'fees'. People want to know the cost of their smallest expenses, but here, on their investment fees, they very often have no idea.

I often ask about fees from people who have investments—or managers who help them with their investments—and typically, the answer is 'I don't know' or 'I'm not sure' or 'I think it's…' Mind you, for a person investing for thirty years or longer, the investment fees, if you're not careful, could easily add up to hundreds of thousands of dollars or more.

Plus, in investing, there isn't just one fee, but layers and layers of fees charged for all kinds of services and things that if people knew, they would really be infuriated.

I guess that's why the financial industry does a very good job of hiding most of the fees in 100-page disclosures written in fine print and in language hard to understand even for a law student. Very often, people think that these 'investments' or this handsome, well-suited financial advisor in the most expensive real estate downtown, doesn't cost them anything (really?). Or they think that it costs some, but it comes out of the investments and 'I don't have to pay anything'. The truth, from someone on the inside of the industry, is that the fees are very real, and they come out of you no matter who pays or what they say.

Always assume that if you don't know what the fees are, they're very high, or they would have mentioned it that the fees are low, so you would compare with others.

But you also don't know others' fees either; you see how complexity breeds complexity and, in this manner, high fees are not visible? Another thing is that the industry doesn't use dollars for fees, mostly, but uses percentages. You're told a 2% fee and you automatically think, well 2% is a small number, not a big deal, right?

Well, 2% of a $500,000 portfolio is $10,000 per year in fees. How does that 2% sound now? Billions of dollars are transferred to the financial industry via high fees. I'm a financial advisor and a fiduciary and I'm not advocating for no fees at all; if there's value provided by the financial advisor or planner of course compensation is warranted, but high unnecessary fees without providing the value of planning or behavioral coaching, take away not just money from client's accounts, but the compounding effects that the money would have had over time. Also, there are many fiduciary advisors that would work for a flat monthly or annual fee, or for a lower percentage fee, especially knowing that the average big brokerage house fees add up to over 2% annual or more, all-in fees.

Cutting that fee by half to around 1%, or often much less, may mean the difference between retiring on time or keep working till your bones fall off.

Investors need to do more research and they'll find out that, while complex and hidden, you can improve your quality of advice while lowering your costs. Under complexity, the big boys of brokerage firms want you not to do that research, but if you do so and reward the firms that are doing right with your business, you both win.

Behavioral Mistakes

People make all of the above mistakes and more, but nothing sets them back as much as the behavioral mistakes, the tricks, the mind plays with them when they think about their money. The behavioral mistakes truly come from financial illiteracy as well as some of the fears, greed and other emotions that encompass humans when they are managing their own money. That's why the best use of an independent advisor is to prevent, coach and educate the client on these behavioral mistakes that everyone is guilty of, including advisors themselves. The more mistakes prevented, the closer clients can get to the theoretical investment returns the market offers. I say theoretical as we've discussed above that most investors do not make—or lag by a lot—what the market offers them.

How investors feel as the market moves up/down

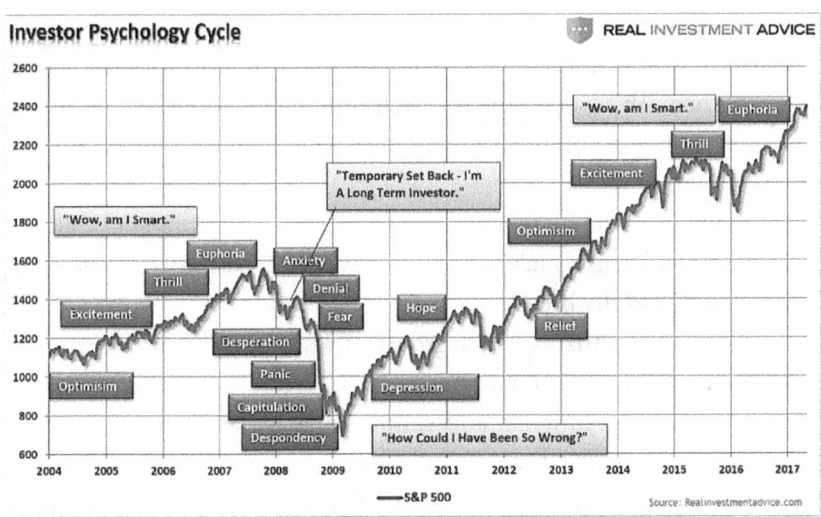

Investor psychology and emotions have a big negative effect on investor

I cannot blame all of these mistakes on the investor, either. Actually, I think the investor is the last to be blamed, mainly for not searching and researching deeper. Most of the blame, in my opinion, lies with the regulators & the big financial firms, both using complexity and revolving doors between them to collude on not doing what's right for the investor.

There's no sugar coating on this as for a very long time, the regulators have had chances to improve on their transparency of services and fees, clarification of titles—like who really deserves to be called a 'Financial Advisor'—further training, education, a clear career path for advisors, and ultimately on the Fiduciary Rule. At every chance that they've gotten, they've kicked the can down the road or created even more complex rules like the most recent one, called 'Best Interest', a continuation of the status quo, that continues to keep the regular investors in the dark. If this doesn't seem to be by design, then I don't know what is. You also can't expect the financial firms or their self-regulatory supervisors (like FINRA) to do much either; it's like the fox regulating itself on not eating too many chickens. It just won't happen. So, what's left is really in the hands of the investors themselves, to educate themselves, do some research on this investing thing—at least as much as they do on buying a car or even a mattress—and see where it takes them.

I really hope to be proven wrong on the regulators soon, and to see some good actions taken with the investors' best interests in mind, but I won't hold my breath.

I also believe that a small group of real financial advisors could make a dent as well. I personally have created a financial literacy course that covers in detail and simple language all that one needs to know about personal finance. It's online, accessible and affordable, and very often I even put it out for free to increase awareness and accessibility.

Many other advisors that I respect do something similar with their blogs, podcasts and videos, giving people ideas and thoughts to improve their financial lives.

It really can be done. Between self-responsibility of investors and the standing up of a few good advisors, I believe people are waking up to understanding personal finance better, making decisions that align with their values and goals and pursuing them thoughtfully. More can be done for sure, but I think a nice base is being layered upon which much more can be built further.

"Investing should be more like watching paint dry or watching grass grow. If you want excitement, take $800 and go to Las Vegas." – Paul Samuelson, Nobel Prize Winner in Economic Sciences, 1970

In summary, your investment plan derives from the bigger picture, which is your comprehensive financial plan. And your financial plan derives from your goals, and your goals derive from your values. Your values derive from who you are and who you want to be. So, start at the very top and work your way down to details while being thoughtful on what really matters to you, and not necessarily what society says should matter to you.

Look at your goals and see what types of accounts are available to you, then fund the accounts with tax benefits first, like 401Ks or IRAs. Investing could also be simpler if you go passive as mentioned above. Diversify your assets, go global and at low cost, such as via index funds and ETFs and don't worry too much what the market does, especially if your goals are long-term ones. **This game of investing is more of a game of patience than a game of skill.** Remember that, since even the most skillful managers lose to just a patient index investor. Use performance enhancers, as mentioned, and a good fiduciary and unbiased advisor could really add value especially if using the right technology to take advantage of certain strategies. At the end, automate them all or as many actions as possible. With the right technology, this is all possible and not only will you be in the 99th percentile of all other investors, but you'll do it with much less stress and with more internal calm while having a peace of mind that you're doing the right thing for yourself and family.

STANDUP

Chapter 10

The Rest of Financial Planning

As we mentioned before, financial planning is the comprehensive viewpoint of everything, both the money aspects and some non-monetary issues of your life.

While many focus on the above, on saving, cash flow, debt management and investing primarily, there are a few more aspects that we'll cover below.

As with everything we've described here, it can be a lot more in-depth and dependent on each family's situation and goals, but I'll give some good summaries that should cover most people's needs. The remaining topics we'll cover are insurance, taxes, educational planning, estate planning and lastly, the different types of financial advisors if you'd ever need one.

Insurance

Insurance is usually a topic either overused by salespeople who are selling unneeded or too expensive insurance using the main tool of 'fear', or underused due to understating its role. I rarely find people who have the right amount of insurance.

So, what is insurance and why do we need it? Insurance is typically needed when there are rare events which can bring catastrophic or severe losses to us. For these rare events, whether accidents or forces of nature, an insurance company takes the risk and we pay a certain premium to move that risk to that company. If something happens, then the company, minus any deductibles, copays etc., pays for the damages. Some insurances are mandated by law, like car or home insurance, and some are optional. Typical insurances are property insurance covering home, auto or belongings, health insurance, life insurance, disability insurance, long-term care insurance and umbrella insurance.

Property insurance is typically the one we are most accustomed to, as it includes the ones typically mandated by law, such as auto and home. You'd want to check what the insurance company pays and what your deductibles or out-of-pocket expenses would be in the case of an accident or home damage. Your premiums or monthly cost depends on many factors including your history, any past claims, where you live, and others.

Your premiums can be lowered or increased based on how much risk you retain (higher deductibles) and how much risk you shift to the insurance company. Flood insurance is typically covered by the federal government, as many insurance companies could not justify the risk of flood vs. what they had to charge for it.

Health insurance is now a very heated topic in US and is the number one concern for many people. It is often offered by your work, but if not, many people can get insurance via healthcare.gov. There are premium subsidies based on your income, and if low income, most of the states have a version of Medicaid where most costs are paid by the state.

There are also high-deductible plans that technically work only in cases of major health concerns as the deductible is too high for normal routine health works, which means that those expenses are paid out-of-pocket.

A saving and investment account known as a Health Savings Account or HSA can be used to save pre-tax money to be used for healthcare if you have a high deductible plan. HSA accounts accrue interest and can also be invested and rolled over to future years if not used, and in addition are not taxed at all if the money is used for healthcare. You can save up to $3500/year per individual or $7000/family in an HSA account.

Prepare for the unforeseen – Pearl Harbor, HI

Life insurance is typically not a pleasant conversation, as it involves discussing death, but it is nevertheless an important conversation, especially if you have dependents that depend on your income. Life insurance is not a windfall or anything like that, not that I know of anyone thinking of it like that, but it is income replacement for the income lost when someone dies, thus it is typically calculated based on the income of the person being insured. How much insurance to purchase depends on how much income you'd want to replace as well as for how long you'd need that income, but a good rule of thumb is between 12-16 times your (the person being insured's) annual income.

So, if your income is $50K a year, a good coverage would be in the $600K - $800K policy. This may seem like a lot to many, which may also seem as very expensive, but if you get coverage when you're young and hopefully not smoking, and getting a term-life policy that covers you for a period of time from ten years to thirty years, it could be surprisingly inexpensive. An example: a $500K policy for an under forty-years-old male, non-smoking and with no health issues could cost under $30/month. There are also more expensive plans like whole-life insurance, but term-life insurance will be the best product for most people; it covers you for a period when you need it while you're building your own assets, and it's inexpensive. That allows you to save and invest for other goals and hopefully after the period of time, you won't need it anymore, as you have either assets to leave to your heirs or you don't have any dependents that depend on your income anymore.

Disability insurance covers someone if they become short-term or long-term disabled. This insurance sometimes is offered from your employer under a group plan, so it's good to check prior to buying your own. There's also disability coverage under the social security government program, if you're expecting to be disabled for a year or longer.

Long-term-care insurance covers nursing home, assisted living and/or adult daycare centers and you can look into it if into your sixties or later.

It tends to be an expensive insurance as the prices for these services continue to go higher but could be helpful if one can cover the premiums.

Lastly, umbrella insurance doesn't cover umbrellas!
It's a term of covering liability—your fault—pertaining to your home or car, or other areas over and above what the usual policies already cover. It tends to be inexpensive, because it typically pays after the other insurances have paid first.

In summary, insurance is a very important part of your financial plan. Don't over insure, but don't skimp either. If underinsured or not insured and something happens, assets or money designated for other goals will have to go to pay for such expenses, thus making a big negative change to your financial path and your objective of reaching your financial goals. Everyone needs health and property insurance and life insurance, when they have dependents. Also be aware of your out-of-pocket expenses—the deductibles, co-insurance, copays, elimination periods when insurance doesn't pay, and so on—so you can know what to expect even if you're insured. Disability, long-term-care and umbrella insurances are less common at a young age, but still good to consider if any of those risks are too high for you and your profession. It's also important where you purchase such insurances.

Lean toward independent sites where you can compare different providers, different plans and more. A few such resources are policygenius.com, selectquote.com or lifequotes.com where you can compare policies, companies and prices online, before making your decision.

Taxes

Taxes are the next big item for many people in financial planning. For some, high-income earners mainly, it's one of the big items and some planning is definitely needed. The goal of tax planning is thinking about your overall financial situation while also looking into legally minimizing unnecessary taxes.

Everyone needs to know the very basics of how income tax works in the US.

The US has a progressive tax system, which means that the tax rates or tax brackets as they're known increase as your income increases.

Major changes happened in the tax code in 2017, which we'll address as well. As with everything we've shared, we'll keep it brief, to the point and to what you really need to know. This is not for you to become an accountant, but just to understand the basic income tax calculations, deductions and credits so you can plan better for your money.

For most people who are hired by a company and get a periodical paycheck, most of the taxes are already withheld even before you get paid. What you see at your paycheck is the NET amount after the deductions. The way those deductions are withheld is basically based on your household size and some IRS rules. This is just meant to be a rough number and every household above some income level is expected to file their taxes prior to April 15 of the following year to see what they exactly owe in taxes.

We'll mainly discuss what happens, and what you need to know about your taxes, as well as what changes you can make throughout the year to minimize your taxes.

In short, when you or your accountant file your taxes before April 15 each year, technically you're taking into consideration your actual situation, your income, taxes, deductions and credits and then comparing those actual taxes with what was withheld during the year. If you overpaid, you'll get a refund, and if you underpaid then you'll owe and have to pay IRS, and that's it. You start with your Gross Income—your W2 that your company provides or other similar forms—and then there are some adjustments to income, basically additions or subtractions, that result in your AGI (Adjusted Gross Income).

Typical additions to income are any interest or dividends that you've received, any business income or loss, any capital gains or losses, and any pension, annuities, IRAs received during the year. Typical subtractions to income are your 401K/IRA deductions, HSAs or Health Savings Account deductions, self-employed health insurance and any student loan interest. After the adjustments and arriving at your AGI, then you get to deduct either a standard deduction or your itemized deductions, whichever is greater, or whichever will give you the largest deduction. With the most recent 'Tax Cuts and Jobs Act' law of 2017, it is expected that the great majority of people (over 90%)

will just take the standard deduction, which was increased to ~$12K for a single household and ~$24K for a married household. It will be slightly increased each year to keep up with inflation.

Most common itemized deductions, if choosing to go that route, are health expenses above a certain hurdle—typically above 10% of your AGI—plus mortgage interest, gifts to charities, and state, local and property taxes capped at a max of $10K.

Once the adjustments & deductions have been made, then you arrive at your taxable income and then, applying the tax brackets, arrive at your tax owed. You're not done yet as there are still some potential tax savings known as tax credits that will reduce your tax owed on a 1:1 ratio. A big tax credit is given for kids, and it was doubled to $2K per child in 2017, and there's also a child and dependent care credit that you could also qualify for if you use any of those services for your child while you're working.

Educational tax credits for college expenses are also major, up to maximum of $2.5K, as well as residential energy credits for mainly alternative energy sources like solar, wind, geothermal and fuel cells. A major, mostly unknown or unused credit is the retirement saver's credit that could be as high as 50% of your savings for retirement, based on your AGI or adjusted gross income. In addition to all the above, in 2017 a new tax deduction was added to small businesses that pass their income to their owners, entities such as LLCs, partnerships or sole proprietors.

While having some limitations, the deduction could be as high as 20% of the net business income, helping entrepreneurs, freelancers and small businesses alike.

All in all, taxes won't ever be eliminated, but with the right knowledge and proper planning they can be reduced and minimized. Some tips to reduce your taxes would be to increase your deductible retirement contributions, fund a 529 education plan for your kids (which is not federally tax deductible, but most states offer state tax benefits), start a small business, go electric, and why not, even have a child if you can or want one?

Also, taxes can be a lot more complex and confusing depending on your income, entities you own, deductions or credits you'd want to take, but for the majority, over 80-90% of people, the above is mostly what happens when taxes are filed.

Now that you know that, you can plan and see what's important to you that may also have a tax benefit. It's almost never recommended to do something just for the tax purpose but looking at the tax consequences or being tax aware is a big component of your comprehensive financial plan.

Educational Planning

Educational planning is another aspect of the comprehensive financial planning that looks at how, where and how much to save and invest for your kids' future education. With the significant tuition increases of the past decades at much higher than inflation, college education has continued to become more and more expensive. Currently, on average, a four-year public university costs over $20K/year, including room and board.

That is over $80K total over the four years of typical college completion and higher if longer than four years. Sure, there are some scholarships and grants that may reduce that sticker cost, but the reality is that the average undergraduate student is graduating with over $35K in student debt. And that is just undergraduate and just an average, so if including more expensive schools or graduate studies, that number moves well into six digits.

College Tuition Fees over time

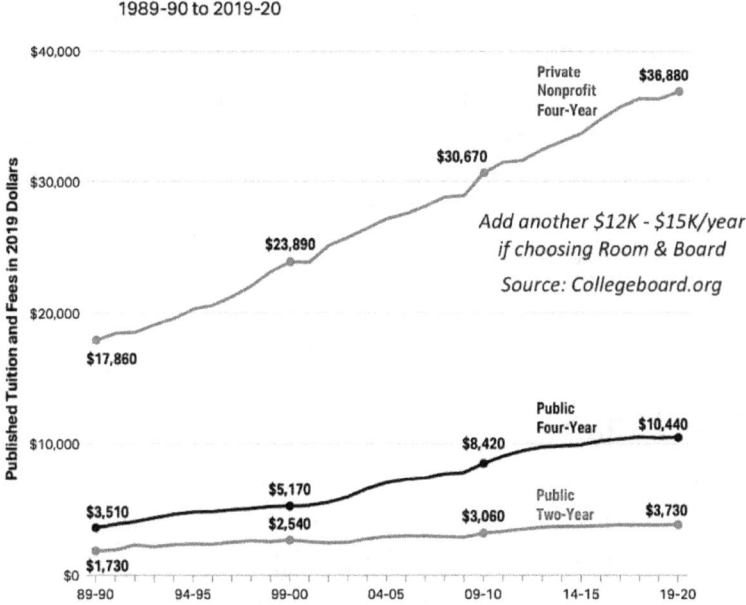

College Tuition has increased at about double the rate of inflation over the past 15+ years

College tuition has been increasing at 5-6% annual for the last fifteen years, according to collegeboard.org, a non-profit that educates and *'connects students to college success'* as it mentions on its webpage. If such tuition growth continues into the future, college costs for a newborn in 2020 will be over $200K for a four-year public university, including room & board, and over $500K for a four-year private one when that newborn is ready to go to college.

Those numbers are high no matter where you stand on the college worthiness or not debate, but there are some things that parents can do to alleviate some of that burden.

One of the major things that parents can do, if affordable, is to start as early as possible to save for their kids' education. If they start early, they can use some of the power of compounding to help them with those costs. They can also get some tax benefits as discussed on the tax section. But moreover, they can even save their own retirement if they do so, as in many cases when parents pay for school and if no investment accounts are in place, they're taking money that could have gone into their retirement funds and thus delaying their own retirement.

Planning ahead has so many benefits, and many are hidden at first.

The 529 Plan

There are several options of where to invest, but typically the best option is known as the 529 plan. The 529 plan is a state-sponsored plan that allows almost anyone to save and invest for education. There are prepaid or investable options, with the main difference that prepaid typically only allows for coverage of in-state-only schools, while the investable option allows for the student to go to any college in the country, and some even outside the country. These 529 plans are either directly sold by the financial institution that the state has contracted with, but sometimes are also sold by brokers who add some additional costs and fees for their work. Many ask how much to invest in these accounts and without saying 'it depends' all the time—as I should, as everything is custom to your specific situation, child's age, school desire, current funds saved, etc,—there's a rule of thumb to apply.

To be able to afford an average state university, tuition only, it means that if you start saving and investing at your child's birth, you should invest about $3K/year or $250/month into the 529 plan. If you aim for your child to attend a private college, then you really need to look into investing at least $6-10K/year or even more, depending on the school. These amounts assume some proper investing of funds as well as attaining reasonable/average rates of returns for the period. Also, if you start later, after birth, the amounts need to be increased and adjusted upward based on how late you start.

There are some other options where you can invest for education, such as Coverdell ESAs or UGMA/UTMA accounts, but they have limitations and are not as popular as the 529 plans. For this purpose, we'll mainly discuss the 529 plans and features.

As mentioned earlier, a 529 plan is a state-sponsored program, where states typically contract with a financial institution to provide the program and the investment choices. The prepaid option typically offered only covers in-state tuition and is usually not used if the student wants to study out of state. On the other hand, the investable option, which is more flexible, will pay for any college anywhere in the country. The maximums you can invest are fairly high and not usually a concern for most people, as you're allowed to invest up to $15K/year per child and you could even pre-fund up to five years upfront or $75K/child per person, or $150K/child if funded by each husband and wife.

There are no income limits to opening and contributing to one, and even friends and relatives can open or contribute to a 529 plan. A little secret that many don't know is that you can have a 529 plan for your child even prior to the child being born!

A 529 plan requires an owner and a beneficiary, but the beneficiary can be changed later, so you can technically open one and name yourself a beneficiary and later change it to your child, thus giving yourself even more compounding time.

Now, not every twenty- or thirty-something may prioritize such when not even having a child and having other needs and goals to save for, but it's an option for the aggressive planners amongst us!

How to select a 529 plan?

First, you'd want to check with your own state and see what is offered. In addition, you'd want to look into any tax benefits that your state is offering as many offer tax deductibility of contributions, at least on state taxes only. Then you'd want to look at the investment options, either the fixed portfolio or the age-based ones, and try to pick the one based on your child's age or length of investment period.

You'd also want to look at the investment fees, as they'll eat up your returns if too high, and aim at something around 0.5% annual or less, unless there are additional tax benefits that you're getting, and even then, you'd not want to go much higher on the fees. You'd want to set up automatic deposits if not doing a large sum, and just let it do its own thing. A good resource for more info on 529 plans is savingforcollege.com.

529 plans have tax benefits if the money is used for education, as intended.

Most states offer state tax deductions with some upper limits, and money in the account grows tax-deferred and comes out tax-free (federal & state) when used for educational expenses. If taken for other than education, there's typically a 10% penalty plus income tax on earnings. As mentioned earlier, you could change the beneficiary to almost anyone in the family, to another child, grandchild or technically any family member with any educational expenses.

With the tax law of 2017 that was passed, 529 plans could now be used for K-12 education expenses in addition to college. You could withdraw up to $10K/year for those K-12 expenses. While it's a benefit, it will allow for less time compounding if you take the money early to pay for those other educational expenses other than college, and the law mostly benefits the ones who start early and have the means to prefund as much as possible.

In closing, 529 plans are tax-advantaged investment vehicles for paying for education. More than thirty states offer additional tax deductibility on contributions, but there is no federal tax benefit on contributions. Money coming out of them and paying for educational expenses is completely tax-free. With the investable plan, you can go anywhere in the country and some out-of-country schools too. You'd want to start as early as possible, automate the deposits, set it and forget it. Also, you can ask friends and relatives to help and contribute too, especially during birthdays if the kids already have enough of the latest toys and gadgets out there.

Estate Planning

Estate planning is a component of a full financial plan that most often is perceived to be useful only for the millionaires or wealthier. While a full-fledged and sophisticated estate plan may be useful and worthy only if you have those millions in the bank, every household needs the basics of an estate plan, or simply planning for when you're gone or incapacitated. That doesn't happen just to the rich, but to everyone, and people need to have the basic legal documents in place to facilitate their wishes.

At the very least, everyone needs a basic Last will, a Living Will, a Power of Attorney (POA) and even a simple revocable trust. These make life easier for you and your loved ones when your health is at its worst—and then, you'll be glad you put the measures in place. These documents will save time and hassle at very emotional moments and you don't want to think about tussling with the legality of something in addition to the human and emotional aspect of what is happening. It is also essential for saving time and money for your loved ones if you pass, avoiding probate, offering creditor protection, and even delivering potential tax benefits.

It is both a convenience and benefit for the living as well as peace of mind for the one having the plan, knowing that your wishes will be followed even when you're gone.

One of the most complex, time-consuming and even expensive processes after death is what's known as Probate, which is the legal and public process (yes, everyone can see what's happening) of retitling assets from the owner that passed on to his or her heirs.

This process is public and can be scrutinized by anyone, but there are ways you can avoid it or reduce the assets that have to go through this process. Estate planning's main function is to make sure most assets avoid the unnecessary public scrutiny of private assets, disbursing assets to the right owners just as the deceased would have wanted to, and doing such with the lowest possible unnecessary transfer taxes.

There are a few ways you can structure your assets in order to avoid probate.

Almost any financial account has a way to have a beneficiary on file.

With any retirement, 401K, IRAs, life insurance policies, annuities and so on, you can simply add a beneficiary to your account, someone who will take that account if something happens to you. You can also do so for any investment and bank account you have.

Secondly, any property that is titled jointly with rights of survivorship, such as between a husband and wife, also bypasses probate as it automatically goes to the surviving member. Lastly, property that has been transferred to a trust, thus doesn't belong to you any longer, also bypasses probate.

These are the main ways that property can bypass the expensive, public and time-consuming process of transferring property from a deceased to his or her heirs.

A Last Will is a relatively simple document, but it could get complex for large estates, where the instructions for the rest of the assets that will go through probate are written.

It is generally typed, witnessed and signed by the creator of the will.

While the Will can be changed at any time, you'd want to make sure to destroy the older versions as well the creator needs to be of 'sound mind' when creating or making such changes, to prevent the creator from being taken advantage of.

A Living Will is a type of a will, narrow in scope, that records your wishes regarding life sustainment, in case you need it, like life support,

CPR, feeding by tubes and similar. It typically designates an 'agent' to make sure that those wishes are followed, and it is signed by you and typically witnessed by two people. A Living Will is needed and helps remove the emotional drama of what the family can do in these situations.

Your own wishes lodged with an agent who follows those wishes, can somewhat clarify the decision-making during these already emotional times.

A Power of Attorney (POA) comes in handy when you'd want to authorize someone to act on your behalf. It can be limited or general, based on the activity for which you'd want to give power to someone, but a General POA is typically given to a very trusted person, like your spouse, to handle and sign for financial accounts if you're not able.

If you travel often or would like someone to act on your behalf, the Power of Attorney can simplify the process by having this individual conduct business and sign documents for you when you're unavailable. A Durable POA also has validity through incapacitation to provide further assistance, signing on your behalf when you're incapacitated. It would come in handy to get access to financial accounts when you're not physically able to.

Trusts are legal documents that authorize one party (the trustee) to manage assets on behalf and for the benefit of one or more beneficiaries. There are three main players in the trust document: the Grantor or the Creator who is creating the trust and also putting money in it; the trustee who manages and has legal title to the assets; and the beneficiary who has the benefit of use of such assets. Trusts come in many shapes and forms, and can be as complex as you'd like them to be, but the main types are revocable and irrevocable, where the prior can be changed and money pulled back into grantor's possession, while the irrevocable cannot and money doesn't belong to the creator any longer.

There are many reasons to create trusts and you may be surprised that you don't need to be super-rich to utilize them or find benefit from them. Trusts allow for the professional management of assets by a fiduciary who has the legal obligation to do what's in the best interest of the beneficiary, while following the instructions as laid out in the trust. They offer creditor protection, especially in terms of the irrevocable ones, as you don't own those assets any longer; they offer privacy, as the assets under trust don't go through probate, and they also offer tax minimization when used properly.

Trusts are also the preferred legal document used by many wealthy families to pass not just assets, but also instructions, guidance and advice to future generations. Many trusts don't ever distribute all their assets to the beneficiaries, but instead pay a certain interest and allow for the money to continue growing for many generations after the creator's death.

As such, it is one of the few instruments that can provide for many generations and allow for the legacy and work of the founder to be continued throughout history.

In summary, everyone, no matter how rich or not, needs an estate plan. The basic documents of Will, Living Will, Power of Attorney, and a Trust can now be easily and affordably set up. You can check either with a local attorney, or even use online resources that can create documents, customize them to your preferences and assist in their filing.

One such is willing.com, that I've also used for my own estate planning. At the end, don't forget the simpler things such as changing beneficiaries when family changes or at least reviewing them periodically.

Sometimes it's the little things that skip through the cracks.

Different Types of Financial Advisors

Wait, there's a difference between advisors? Yes, and at times, a big one. Not all 'financial advisors' are built the same, as they go by different titles, have different accreditations, are registered by different regulators and much more, but I'll do my best to describe all that you need to know so that you can make an informed decision, just in case you ever need personalized financial advice more than what's described in this book.

Why the titles matter more than you think

As I've mentioned in other parts of this book, the financial industry is a complex one; on purpose or not is another discussion, but nothing confuses investors more than just the simple titles that advisors carry. Some call themselves 'wealth managers', some are just 'VPs', some are 'financial representatives' or 'registered representatives', while at times you may find 'Investment manager' or 'Investment Advisor Representative'.

But nothing confuses people more than just the common 'financial advisor' title. That title that is so commonly used does not have much meaning because everyone in the financial advisory or financial sales industry can currently use it, as it is not regulated. Even my dog can be a 'financial advisor'; nothing is required of him to carry that title, although I have to say, I probably wouldn't accept his advice or buy whatever he's selling!

'Financial Advisor' is a title that is not just reserved for 'advisors' as the name notes, but also for pure financial salespeople selling a financial product and not offering advice at all. While that may not seem big to you now, you'll see how just that title matters and confuses people on who is giving advice and who is selling something.

Still, you may say, ok, but who cares? You should, if you want to make sure you get to keep more of your money…the difference could easily be in the hundreds of thousands of dollars over a long period of investing, such as how it impacts on your retirement savings.

Why am I making such a big deal about this? It is because if the people or investors cannot identify who they're dealing with and what's being offered, either a service (advice) or a product (sales), it will make a huge difference to what you as the investor receive at the very end.

Are their incentives aligned with yours?

The big difference between different 'financial advisors' is the incentives they have to provide to you as well as the fees that are charged.

If you cannot identify well if one is giving you unbiased advice vs. selling you a financial product, that will make all the difference in the service you get, the product you're sold and eventually the outcomes down the road from those investments that you bought. This is what's known as the fiduciary vs. suitability debate in financial advising, but even that doesn't mean much to most people, so I'll discuss another real-life scenario that will better convey the point.

So, let's take an example, to better illustrate this. You'd like to purchase a new car, have done some research and would like to take a look at the new Honda sedan that just came out. You know of a nearby Honda dealer and go to visit it and check it out. A person greets you, and introduces herself and asks you about your visit and what specifically you may be looking for and how she could help you. You mention that you've come to take a look at the new Honda sedan. The car salesperson offers assistance in providing answers for any question you may have, including a test drive. So far, so good.

Now, let's twist the situation a bit. What would happen if you suddenly start asking questions about other cars like Toyotas or BMWs at the Honda dealership? Well, you'd say, I'm not that stupid, I can't expect answers on such questions as this is a Honda dealership, and doesn't sell Toyotas or BMWs. True and true, and this is a suitability example in financial advice, where you mostly know what you want and go to a salesperson to ask a few questions about the product and to buy and facilitate the transaction.

Nothing wrong with it in this scenario, and typically that's how we buy cars, BUT we definitely know that the salesperson is on the dealer's side.

We know they will try to get the best price for themselves and the dealer, while you'll try to negotiate and get the best price for yourself, kind of 'buyer beware'.

Most people know that's how this operates, so you do lots of research on it, on the car, features, on pricing, what others have paid etc. and go prepared to make a deal, but again you know that you're not on the same side of the table as the dealer, who'll aim to first get you to buy there and secondly to buy at the highest possible price that they can potentially sell you. It's known, expected and people are prepared for it. It is also how we operate with many other retailers, where we know what we want, there's available information and we can do or have already done research on it.

The financially illiterate can't see they're screwed

It is completely different with investment advising or trying to get financial advice. First, most people are not well versed in investing and in the variety of the products and services that are offered. As mentioned above, the titles of people helping you don't seem to make a difference either, especially if anyone can carry that title.

Next, investing is intangible; you can't 'test drive' or check under the hood or even see how it looks, and you can't touch it or feel it. Research is very complex, comes in different shapes and forms and media, and people who talk about investments all come and go and most often say different things too, so you're not sure who or what to believe out there.

So, what happens is that most people go with their gut feeling, as that's the only thing that's left if you're not financially literate or haven't done a ton of research on the topic. When you go with your gut feeling, without much research, knowledge, testing or even past experiences to base it on, most people tend to be drawn to what's familiar, big known brands and the big financial institutions and their representatives.

The problem now is that your research and guidance that you had prior to buying your car doesn't exist at all in investing, so it's the equivalent to going to 'Best Cars Dealership' where you're not sure what car brand you're buying or what it looks like; you just have to trust the company and the person behind the desk that it's a good car and the best for you, or so he says. You don't seem to pay for it any money up-front, make your deposit for the investment and hope for the best. The keyword in all this is 'trust', as when you only trust without verifying, that opens the door for abuse. Under the suitability rule, or the rule that brokers operate, this product doesn't have to be the best for you, it just has to fit you based on certain parameters. Let me rephrase it with the car example. At the 'Best Cars dealership', the salesperson doesn't have to give you the best car they have or could have, but they give you a car that drives and that is OK, knowing that there are better and even cheaper cars out there that could fit you much better. But they aren't obligated to give you that and they'll give you whatever they want to sell off the lot. And since you don't know how investments work and can't see or touch them, you don't know you just got a crappy investment. Since it is complex and opaque, the worst or mediocre cars could be sold as best cars at the 'Best Cars Dealership'; of course, they'll say we only have the best cars. See, it's in our name!

See how it works? This system has plenty of conflicts of interests, and you can notice that the broker under the suitability rule works for his company and is just simply completing a transaction with you, regardless of what is best for you.

He also most often gets compensated by his employer via commissions for your investments and transactions, so you don't get to see the details of the fees or what products pay what fees or other incentives to the broker. It is a third party that is paying for your supposed advice; how could that even work?

Oh, it works great!

Just not for you.

***

As you can see from my analogy with cars, something that comes so natural to most of us, it's not so easy with the buying, selling or getting help with investments.

The main difference is the knowledge that people have, stories they have heard, and even history and brand recognition. With so many items we purchase, say cars, electronics, clothes, food etc., we have come into contact with them and either done deep research or just by using them, we get accustomed, learn and get to know what they are. With investments not so much.

Fiduciary: Putting clients' interests first

So, for something like investing, another system that already exists is much more efficient and better for the client. This system is known as the fiduciary duty, where the advisor is obligated by law to put clients' interests first and do what's best for the client, disclose fees and any potential conflicts in detail and try to minimize or completely remove those conflicts. A subset of these advisors are also known as 'Fee-Only' or Registered Investment Advisors (RIA) as they receive fees only from their clients as compensation, <u>and from no one else</u> which is not to be confused with 'Fee-Based' which is used by the dually-registered advisors, both registered as brokers and advisors, mentioned below. This fiduciary system allows the professional advisor to take responsibility and provide the best advice and thus get or suggest the best available products for the client. There is a direct relationship of paying for service between client and advisor, where the client directly pays the advisor for this advice, and the advisor is not paid by any third party. While there are conflicts of interests in any business where you deal with clients, under such a system of transparency and directly paying your advisor, and knowing no one else is paying him for advice to you, you're removing most of the worst incentives that salespeople have to put you in a crappy or mediocre investment. You are getting rid of the outside influence and money of a third and unrelated party.

Do due diligence with any advisor you choose

Even if you choose a fiduciary advisor or 'fee-only', there's still some more work to do into identifying what they offer, their services, their fees and how they can actually work and help you. As with any business, you still have to do some research on them, their background, experience, and accreditations and how willing or able they are to be working with you, and at what cost. Lastly, as with any business or person, not every broker is bad and not every fiduciary advisor is good. It's still individual people and businesses that can take many forms and shapes, but at least now you know their motivations and incentives and have a better idea about how to choose and what to look and ask for.

And if the above weren't complex enough—I joke, I joke—most of the big-name investment firms you know and recognize operate under dual registration, where the 'advisor' is both a broker as well as an investment advisor. He can act in both positions, as s/he sees fit, and typically can be both a broker and an advisor to the same client, getting paid both commissions and fees. Many call this 'dual hatting' where the advisor chooses which 'hat' to wear based on the situation, confusing most people about what they're getting or paying for. Again, many advisors in any of the mentioned business models are overall good people who want to do well, but the incentives are not aligned to let them do well even if they wanted to.

Get help from a fiduciary advisor to make you see the forest beyond just the tree in front of you – Stanley Park, Vancouver, Canada

Check 'all-in' fees

Typically, what happens under this complex environment is a lot of product selling and not much advice, not fiduciary anyways. Under a system like this where most people—more than half—don't know what fees they're paying or believe that there are no fees and that their service is free, you better believe that the service is not free. And when you're not sure what it is, it usually is too high. After a wall of complexity and 'don't worry, you're not paying me' excuses hide very high and unjustifiable multi-layers of fees.

Investment fees are like onions, with many layers and they make you cry even more as you peel them one by one. Under a broker model, you typically get put into mutual funds that charge almost 5%+ upfront commission—or on a fund-share class that pays that commission (typically 1%) annually to the broker—to purchase them.

Typical Fees	Broker / MF1	Broker / MF2	Fiduciary Advisor
Sales/commissions (paid upfront or backend)	5.75%	5.75%	None
Investment Mgmt. fees (internal)	0.69%	0.85%	0.07%
Turnover ratio (inside-fund trading)	0.3%	0.76%	0.03%
Performance Enhancers/ Technology (ETFs, auto-rebalance, tax-loss harvesting, tax location)	Benefit not offered	Benefit not offered	0.25%
12B-1 Fees / Advisor (annual)	0.25%	0.25%	1.00%
Annual Totals (over a 5-year period)	**2.24%**	**2.86%**	**1.35%**

Comparing fees of a broker using mutual funds (MF) vs. a fiduciary, fee-only advisor. These fees are taken from a real case, but also very typical.

Plus, you have the annual investment management fees that go to the investment manager of the mutual fund (another 0.5%-1.5%+ annual, depending on fund), plus 12B-1 fees (typically 0.25% annual or more depending on the mutual fund share class) that go to the broker every year you keep the mutual fund. Then there are hidden fees like turnover, unnecessary taxes and inside fund costs of trading that could go as high as 1% for an active trading and high turnover fund. These costs, either paid directly or indirectly by the investor, go even higher under annuity type of investments that add their own layers of insurance (Mortality & Expense Ratio), administration and other miscellaneous fees known as 'riders'. All-in fees including broker fee plus mutual funds used and turnover/tax inefficiency for broker-sold products could vary from as low as 2%+ annual, up to as high as 3.5% annual or more in the annuity models.

On the other hand, many independent RIAs (fiduciary, fee-only advisors) charge in the 1% annual range or lower, with some higher fees for smaller balances and/or lower fees for higher balances over $1M. Plus most of them use index funds and ETFs that are very inexpensive. Many broad-based ETFs' fees are now below 0.1% annual.

Also, let's not just focus on the fees alone, but the value of the services as well.

Many RIAs offer comprehensive financial planning that, as discussed before, is a more in-depth review of all the facets of someone's financials, matching values and goals with your money while continuously keeping your plan and goals up to date.

But still, do your homework, and ask and get to know how exactly your advisor is compensated, by whom, and what services will be provided together with that, and if he's going to be a fiduciary to you or not and <u>get that in writing</u>.

Still, the problem with fees is that they don't work how we're used to. In real 'tangible' life, we're used to associate higher costs or prices with better utility, higher quality products and overall better products. That's why we pay more for those and justify the cost by thinking of the extra benefits we receive. In investing, it doesn't work like that and also more and more research proves the opposite, that high fees have an adverse effect on performance, so the more you pay the less you get. It makes sense if you think that most active funds don't beat the average stock market index, while charging you more for it.

You're not getting any benefits; actually, you're getting fewer benefits as you pay more for it. Even a 0.5% or 1% annual difference in fees could mean thousands or hundreds of thousands of dollars lost over a lifetime of investing. If this weren't complex and intangible, no one would have paid Neiman Marcus prices for a Walmart-sold product, but in investing it happens daily and people pay for it with real dollars that could have instead gone into a better retirement or faster achievement of their goals.

What can be done about it?

As you get through understanding this and maybe doing some more research on your own, you'll get to realize that there's a lot more value in focusing on overall planning and not the nitty gritty of stock investing. If you need an advisor to guide you, make sure you understand who they are, what services they offer, what their incentives are and how they're compensated. Make sure you hire a fiduciary, someone who's planning-focused and who will work with you, educate you along the way and align their interests with yours.

Know and ask about fees and choose and pay for the services that add value to you. Demand use of technology, ease of use and the different enhancers that are available. Make sure there's a fit and that the advisor will be around for a while too, as the majority of advisors now are over fifty-five years old, according to research by Cerulli Associates.

There are other new forms of advisory businesses coming up that further align the interests with their clients' while making services available to many more.

Many advisors, like myself, focus on education and planning, with transparent fees that could be paid not just from investments. You could pay monthly fees, flat annual fees, or even hourly fees for the service and that makes this system more accessible to people who don't have any investments or are just starting out. The move away from commissions, sales and product focus is intensifying and there's a new breed of advisors forming, getting stronger, making noise and disrupting the current non-fiduciary and sales-oriented financial industry. I'm proud to be part of this group of independent registered investment advisors (RIAs) focused on doing what's best for the client. Being a fiduciary means aligning interests with clients, focusing on planning and not just investments, helping clients with their goals and life-planning, all enhanced by technology. It also means charging reasonable and transparent fees and understanding that 'doing what's right' matters a lot more than making a couple of extra bucks.

STANDUP

Chapter 11

All about RVing

This is probably the section you've been waiting for; I know, me too. RVing brought about the uniqueness of our whole trip and we did it fifteen months full-time and uninterrupted, quite long enough to get a feeling for what life could be like in a nomadic state.

Granted, this is not your 1800s nomadic, traveling by foot and enduring all the elements, but still many of the feelings and experiences are much more enhanced when you're on the road, sleeping in a vehicle and driving to new places almost every 5-7 days. RVing was what made this trip and my passion to give back and educate much more enjoyable, fun and adventurous. So, let's get in. I'll lay out most of what we learned, most of our memorable stories and places, but mainly how we felt about it and what we learned that we all could use in other areas of our life and business.

Spoiler alert; you'll want to do it too.

Travel

Both my wife and I have been traveling long ago in our adult lives. We're immigrants to US and our trips didn't stop at visiting many areas of the world and US, but US trips were sparse here and there, certain areas in the North East and Southeast and very limited on the west coast, north west and the middle of US. One of the rules we set on early was that we would visit all US states, or we'd try at the minimum to aim for the continental US.

After we decided that we would do this, and we would do it via an RV, a lot of research went into this. What type of RV, used or new, how long, what options, towing a car or not, pricing, financing and more were the thoughts going on. But we started, as I usually do, with the big picture, covering major concerns then trying to optimize as we moved forward. About nine months before leaving for our RV tour, we took a trip to Texas, some for fun and some for research. We had already looked up and found out from other RVers and bloggers that there was this huge RV dealership in Texas.

Well, as Texas is big, so was this dealer!

We were given golf carts to go around and check different RVs, spending almost six hours doing just that. For the beginners, as we were, we learned early that there were three main RV classes: A class, B Class and C class. The A class would be the really bigger RVs, with many amenities and luxuries. The B class would be your smaller, van-type RVs where the Mercedes diesel chassis is king, and the C class would be bigger than the B class, smaller than the A class but with fewer amenities and typically cheaper than both A & B classes. Don't ask me why; I don't know why the classes are like that.

We did most of our hands-on homework at this same Texas place, getting a feel of different RVs, the layouts, the beds, kitchen and storage options. It's like a kid at a candy store, but you're prepping yourself to order a candy that you've never had before and can't really get a taste of.

You have to get a feeling by just looking at it and going nowhere. Good luck with that.

Budgeting

We also had a budget in mind, as we didn't want to surpass certain costs of RVing and traveling. Early on, after some research on used

RVs and potential problems, we decided that we were going to buy a new RV and finance it. After reading mainly horror stories about people having issues with RVs, from roof leaks to bathroom problems, to mechanics, electric and electronics, we decided we were not handy enough to take care of such problems if they happened to us. A new RV, made up of two parts, a vehicle chassis (typically Ford) and a 'home component' both came with warranties.

It was one year of warranty on the home part, including pretty much anything that could go wrong on any living components, and a five-year warranty on the vehicle parts provided by the car manufacturer as typical with most cars and trucks. We were planning to have the trip last for about a year, so the warranties covered us for almost anything that could go wrong. I created a spreadsheet, of course, with costs of financing, down-payment requirements, our monthly payment as well as a rough estimate of our monthly traveled miles and an average miles/gallon (mpg) multiplied by an average national cost of a gallon of gasoline. The numbers, in hindsight, were very close to what we encountered.

From my research, a V10 Ford gasoline engine would average around 8-12 miles per gallon. Since we decided that we would also tow a small car, I opted for the low end of the range, 8 mpg, for my calculations. And you complain about your vehicle doing twenty miles to the gallon? Welcome to RV world.

Research

We (especially Julieth) did a lot of reading and research on RVs on the ground in Texas, but also on the Internet. You may not become an RV expert in a few months, but you read enough stories and personal experiences from other RVers, and you start to get the picture. What we got was that pretty much any RV had its own problems; some brands were worse than others with more problems, but no brand was perfect. They almost used similar vehicle chassis and engines for similar types of RVs, and then the RV manufacturers would outfit, create the structure, build the insides and have the different options and layouts.

We wanted to keep our budget in check and thus were looking at the C class, which provided enough space for our long trip, but also wasn't too expensive. The B class, which I liked a lot from the driving as well as fuel economy stance—most ran on Mercedes diesel chassis—didn't convince us on the size; they ran from twenty to twenty-five-feet long and had no slides and were very small inside. Looking back from what we learned, we maybe could have pulled it off in a Class B, but maybe for another time.

The Class A were big, roomy and also more expensive. Some look like buses and some were slightly smaller, but we were both 'scared' from the high price as well as the feel of driving it. I sat inside a Class A at the Texas dealer and thought to myself: 'How would I even drive this thing?' Our research was moving along, and we had identified couple of brands we were OK with, depending on their layouts and storage space we were looking for. We didn't have much stuff to store, just our belongings and kitchen stuff and suchlike, and we were already living in a relatively small apartment. But storage is very valuable in an RV, the more the better. We also had two foldable mountain bikes that we wanted to take with us and store inside and looking for a large storage compartment was also important. We decided to visit the largest RV show in the Northeast, in Hershey, PA, and look up close at the RVs we had researched.

And maybe, if we found the right deal, we might buy there as well.

Buying

We read that many people buying new RVs were doing so at the RV shows, where you could compare brands, options, layouts and pricing all in the same area. It sounded great for us to visit and see what it was all about. At the Hershey Park RV Show we visited the brands we were looking at, but for one reason or another, couldn't find the layout and storage capacity we were looking for, and when we did, the pricing wasn't to our satisfaction.

Then, almost giving up on the show, toward the last couple hours of the last day of the show, we visited the THOR RV brand. We had done some research on the THOR and had an idea that it was decent, but mainly among the more expensive models.

In the last couple of years, they had introduced a new version that took some of the benefits of the A class (decent size, space and layout) and blended that with the price consciousness and the capacity of the C class. Smartly, they had called this combination model A.C.E for A-Class, C-Class, Evolution. The price for the space provided was very reasonable, as we had found smaller RVs that were more expensive, so we decided to go in and take a deeper look. After an hour or so of reviewing the most important things of the RV, the layout, the space, the price and the overall feeling of it, we…decided to buy it!

But of course, that was not without further negotiating on the price, which supposedly was already discounted for the show. And here's the little secret on RV prices; the MSRP is almost worthless and just a high-price anchor that will make you feel much better when you get a lower price. You can say that's common for many car manufacturers, but I guarantee you, they're nothing compared to the way RVs are priced. And if you happen to go to one dealer vs. another, it could mean tens of thousands of dollars in price differential.

We had all our knowledge from the Texas dealer—which I keep repeating here due to our great experience and learning we got there. Their name is 'Motor Home Specialist' located in Alvarado, Texas, of off I-35 about fifty minutes south of Dallas. We came prepared with the knowledge that MSRP means nothing, but an anchor we could use to request percentage discounts of off it. At the minimum, a 25%

discount of MSRP was almost a guarantee on any unit that we checked at the Texas dealer. Sometimes, you could find units with 30% or even higher, all the way up to 40% off MSRP. It depended on the unit and their demand etc., but it gave us a ballpark to aim for. The unit we wanted was already about 28% off MSRP with major promotions around it as 'Show Only Pricing' etc, meaning that this was a real deal, but I knew it wasn't the best we could get.

After some firm negotiation at the last hour of the last day of the show, we got almost 40% off the MSRP, a price that we felt was good and under our budget. And they also had special financing right there, for which we got approved and the terms were much lower than we had found on our own. So overall, I would say a good buy.

We were happy, until that night when one of us—wink, wink Julieth—had a minor episode of buyer's remorse, but overall nothing that we couldn't pass. We got the RV, yeahhhh!

Picking up the RV

From buying the RV at the show till actually picking it up was over a month or more. They had to find the right RV (yeah, I know, they sold us a theoretical RV), with the right paint stripe which I believe was the only option on our unit, then bring it to a dealer where we could pick it up. Almost five weeks later, we were told the RV was ready for pick up.

We were excited, as this was getting real as well as a bit frightening, as this was getting real! We were given the closest dealer to us, the Camping World in Hanover, PA. We had read a lot of reviews on different RV dealers, and Camping World wasn't the most highly rated, but that's where we got the best deal, so what could possibly go wrong now?

We set up the appointment to pick it up and I remember it as now there was heavy rain that day, on and off. We went to the dealer and it seemed they were already very busy with other people from the show, all picking up their own RVs. Now, a bit of intro here, the picking up of an RV is not the same as that of a car; at least, we expected more of a difference there and had set aside much time to be shown what was what with our new arrival. This would be the time where you'd get shown most or all of the functions of the RV, especially of the house portion. For newbies like us, it was a day to absorb the most info from a real RV professional and ask as many questions as possible.

That may not go too well with someone not really up to newbie questions about RVs or just someone like us, atypical for buying an RV, since most are old and somewhat experienced with RVing. We were assigned a team member of Camping World who would show us the unit, the features and whatever else we needed to know. It was expected to be a short review of just about everything—our RV's complete lowdown, if you like, given that we were total newbies and honestly didn't know the first thing yet.

Well, you guessed it, after all my preamble; our complete A-Z lowdown felt like it was not long or thorough enough to absorb all we needed to know about the RV, but we felt right away that this team member had already 'seen enough for the day'.

He looked tiredly at the people, the other staff and probably even at himself that moment he took us to our new RV. He was really only envisaging getting off home.

The RV seemed nice, had that desirable new car smell, and we went over many of the features with him, while I was recording to remember stuff for later. But a situation quickly arose when this salesperson, now visibly annoyed by our questions, started to show obvious signs of frustration and even giving answers full of attitude. After enduring his rudeness for a while, I thought this wasn't supposed to be like that and I finally asked him to leave, as I didn't want to deal with him any longer but asked for another person to finish what he started. He was really angry from the very beginning, and even looked down at us as a 'couple of kids' not knowing what we were doing buying an RV. The fact was, we were relatively a couple of clueless kids—but we were excited and committed, and we really wanted a salesperson who shared in our joy. Was that so wrong a thing to hope for?

The next person was more reasonable, so we took couple breaths to recover from the tense situation and continued with the review. We finalized with him, now wanting it to end and just get out of there. We got the keys, and I got in and followed Julieth driving the other car into a campground where we were going to stay the night, about 45 minutes away. It was a little tense driving the largest vehicle I had ever driven, but I got in and we drove away. The journey had begun.

The trip begins

We drove and camped with the RV few other times that fall of 2016, but it was already starting to get cold and winter was coming. We decided to park it for the season at a campground in PA and then whenever ready, go and pick it up when we were ready to get going. Our trip was supposed to start in mid-January 2017, but I got really sick after a trip from South Korea, thus we had to postpone it for about two weeks.

We finally left for our trip on February 7th, 2017.

It was a weird feeling leaving, as we weren't going *anywhere* specific, but at the same time we were planning to go *everywhere*, so the saying 'nowhere, but everywhere' comes in mind. We purged many of our belongings, and as we did so, clothes and kitchen stuff, and goodwill donation boxes were getting piled up—and these would keep on coming even during our trip. Downsizing is imperative when living fulltime in an RV. So, when it was time to go finally, we got a small U-Haul, got our few belongings and some kitchen and other items and drove to the dealership.

Julieth fully organized this, with me mainly being just the 'muscle'. Following on from first picking it up, we'd had the RV back at the dealership for some minor fixings (yep, fixings on a brand-new RV) since December and it had been there for almost two months—and thus, we 'moved home' at the RV dealer's parking lot.

Once all in, we moved into a campground nearby where we would get ourselves accommodated and empty all the boxes into their places and such.

What we weren't following too closely was that a storm was moving into the area, and on our first night we got snowed in at least four inches. Well, it was February after all. No running water since we had the RV still winterized so the pipes wouldn't freeze, and now there was snow outside. While it seemed we were alone in a large empty RV park, we started our RV adventure.

The little one

In our research, we found out that there were a few different ways we could drive an RV as well as a vehicle to move around cities. We could get a truck/SUV and pull a non-motorized 'home part', also known as a trailer or 5th wheel. We could get a small RV (van type) that we could drive in towns. Or, we could pull a car behind a large RV. Through our research, and not already having a truck/SUV, the most convenient, cheaper, spacious and easy way was to tow a car behind. Some more research went into the type of car and whether we would tow it on its own wheels, all four or two on the ground, or if we would have a platform where the car would sit on top. If towing with its own wheels, then more research had to be done on the type of car that the manufacturer allowed to be towed and if so, how. We finally decided on a Fiat 500 with a manual transmission.

We liked manual cars already, but also, Fiat allowed it to be towed flat on all 4 wheels, with the transmission in neutral and no other restrictions. We named our Fiat 'The Little One' as it's a fairly small coupe, but it still fits four adults. We also named the RV 'Minerva' from the Roman goddess of wisdom, arts, trade and strategy.

We thought our trip represented 'knowledge in motion' while creating the basis for business, strategy and future growth, and maybe subconsciously we wanted the protection of an ancient Roman goddess to watch over these amateurs going around the country. With both cars already finalized, all we had to do was 'connect them'. That's another part where a connection plate was attached to the towed Fiat, then through a tow bar connected to the RV. In many states, brakes were needed on the tow car to operate concurrently with the brakes in the RV, seemingly a professional job that we took care of it at an RV dealer. We were now connected and ready to drive.

Driving & parking it

The first time I drove the RV with the Fiat towed behind, it felt really weird. Driving a 'big house' from a small seat where you controlled everything, just like a pilot in an airplane, well, you get the point. While I was experienced in driving, I had never driven anything that long and wide. The RV itself was thirty-two feet long and together with the tow bar and the Fiat behind us, we were almost fifty feet long. I had to make really wide turns and then hope and pray that the little one followed along and didn't jump a sidewalk or so.

You can tell a rookie RV driver by the way he or she drives. The first few drives until I got the hang of it, I could notice I would come and almost touch the right white line, don't know why, but maybe over-compensating for thinking that it was too wide and didn't want to block two lanes, mine and the one on the left!

The first couple of months, I would almost always drive on the right lane and at speed limit or at times even lower, depending on the incline or the road. The first long trip from PA toward our first event at Virginia Tech University I got the good idea of how trucking really feels. Big trucks would pass me on the left and 'push' me right as they came and then 'pull' me left as they passed. The wind tunnel that was forming either when they were coming or when they were passing was something I had to get used to.

But after a while, you know how much of a push or pull you get and then you could expect and manage it by doing the opposite so you could stay in lane. After the first few months, I was almost accommodated to all the quirks I had to know about driving a fifty-foot, 30,000 pounds combined machine.

The same with parking it. At a campground where we would stay for a few days, we would typically disconnect the little one and then park. Parking had its own system too. Our RV had hydraulic jacks that would help level the RV, which is very important, especially for proper operation of appliances. I would initially park at a level area, making sure to be in proximity to the connections for water, electricity and sewerage, then go outside and put the wooden boards underneath the jacks for better support—as well as not to have the jacks overextend as that would cause potential wobbling when inside or even a potential for bending or breaking of a jack. Once the wooden pieces that I had cut at a Home Depot were underneath the jacks, then I would signal Julieth to lower the jacks while I observed their positioning on top of the wooden pieces. I would then start to connect the electricity with the campground via our own cables, as well as the water from the water supply on each site, while Julieth would take care of the inside, extend the one long slide we had and put other things in their place. I typically wouldn't connect the sewer yet and tried to only connect it when needed. This was at a typical RV park that provided 'full hook-ups' which means the electrical supply, water and sewer.

In other places that either didn't have water or sewer, we would just connect the electric… or if nothing, then there was nothing to connect! The RV came with a generator that we could use to power everything that would run on gasoline from the gas tank, a fifty-gallon fresh water tank for showering or washing dishes, a forty-gallon gray water tank where sink & shower water collected, and a thirty-gallon black water tank where toilet water accrued.

It also had an eighty-gallon gas tank capacity that always reminded me when I filled it up with gas. The gas trips had to be planned well in advance and we frequented gas stations that catered to RVers, that typically had larger lots and more space to turn without the need to back up (Flying J & Pilot brands comes in mind), which I couldn't do while connected to the little one. The RV place that installed the tow bar and connection of the RV with the little one told me that if I needed to back up, I had to disconnect first.

But in all the thousands of miles and hundreds of gas station stops I only had to disconnect once where I couldn't turn as it was too tight, and I had to back up. All in all, driving it, parking it and even filling it with gas required full attention and I had my game face all the time; no time to slack when driving the big Minerva.

The map & planning

We had a plan in mind, but it was very vague at first.

It was to drive through and visit all fifty states, reaching out to all or most colleges and universities in our path about my financial literacy seminar and do it all in a year or so.

At the time of the launch, we had secured only one seminar, through a connection and friend, at the Virginia Tech in Virginia. The rest we would email and connect with while on the go. That's a point that I have made and will further make on planning. You can never be 100% certain or 'planned', as whatever you do will never all be known ahead, so you'd have to move with anything over 50%. We knew what we wanted to do, how and a rough where, and that was more than enough to get going. I bet if we waited for further details to be completed, we would have never done it. Since it was still winter and we got a quick taste of it with the first snow on our first week, the plan was to move south, first at Virginia Tech and then further south from there. I would research universities on our path and cold email the directors or anyone in charge of the 'Career Center' of the universities and colleges. I believed that it was the responsibility of the 'Career Centers' of the universities to prepare the students for life after school.

Financial Literacy Event at Virginia Tech – Blacksburg, VA

Since financial literacy and my seminar was all about how to save, invest and overall manage financial life after school, I thought that was a more focused target, rather than just emailing random people at the school. Over time, I got better and faster at research, looking at the next 2-3 states where we would move in the next month or so and email them with my potential time frame that I would be in the area. We moved rather quickly from Virginia toward Florida trying to get away from cold weather. Florida was good to us, and we visited and presented in two schools there, at University of Miami and then on the west coast at Eckerd College, visited the Keys and warmed up in sunny weather.

As the summer was approaching, we decided to loop back up north but first checking New Orleans, Atlanta, Nashville and Pittsburgh. Moving during summer toward the north-east was more enjoyable than the colder months we'd left behind when up there.

Eventually, we had the summer and fall to move cross-country and hopefully not hit any harsh colder weather as we navigated west. I can talk and talk about our trip, but as they say, a picture is worth a thousand words. Here is where we traveled and our path (below). We would make the route about 2-3 months in advance, and I would contact schools 1-2 months ahead. We would look for campgrounds about 2-3 weeks ahead. It was somewhat a schedule that allowed us to plan, but also leave room for spontaneity; after all, we didn't have to follow a particular route, highway or path.

We were making our own. Literally.

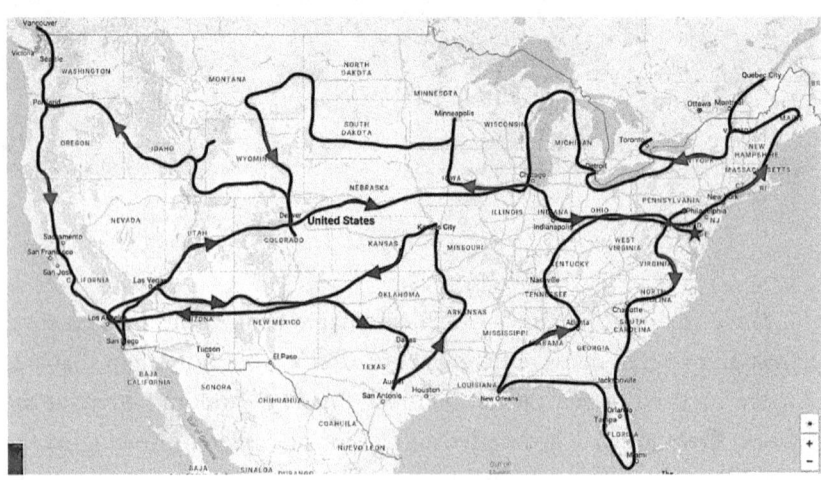

Our travels covered pretty much all of US

Warranty at work

After the fact, I still think we did better that we got a new RV. For many others, maybe they'll think it's a waste of money or not worth it to spend that much, but for us novices knowing that all the stuff where we had no idea how it worked was covered under warranty made a difference. It made a monetary difference, that we didn't have to worry about what it would cost to fix something, but also a mindset and overall calmness that would allow us to focus on doing our work and traveling, rather than what if this thing went wrong or not. And we did use the warranty, at least on three major occasions where we scheduled many little things to be fixed all at once. We kept lists of items, sometimes as small as a USB outlet not working, so that on our next 'warranty work' we could take care of it.

We did warranty work in three states, Pennsylvania, Florida and Illinois, where we took care of different things that either malfunctioned or weren't working properly.

You may ask 'Are most RVs this crappy?' and the answer is that at the beginning, many things move and shake (duhhh) and many things show if a problem or not after a few months of use. Then they get fixed and typically the initial problems subside, or so we're told; we don't have the RV any longer to confirm what happens after.

To anyone that doesn't know anything about RVs or undertaking something similar, look into it as the value of warranty being more of a peace of mind than anything else.

When you're on the road and don't know where you'll be parking or sleeping next, you'd want to know that if something goes wrong, it is covered. Also, most large RV dealerships that have repair and maintenance shops work directly with the manufacturer, so you don't have to do any paperwork etc. but just show up with your problem and hopefully it will be taken care in a reasonable amount of time. Usually, it takes longer than you think, especially if they need parts that they don't have, but the one time in Florida where we almost burned the RV down due to bad wiring, we got it fixed on the same day, while the other times we had to schedule it and it took longer than a week. Sometimes (we were told) it could even take months depending on what the problem was.

Sleeping in it

The first few nights, we had to get used to sleeping in it. An RV is fairly poorly insulated compared to a home, and you can hear almost all outside noises. The very first night during a windy and cold night on the first PA campground, we heard footsteps noises on the roof.

Wow, I thought, *someone is on top of our RV, but why?* It really sounded like footsteps, so I went outside and armed with a baseball bat and another 'undisclosed weapon', climbing the back ladder to the roof. To my pleasant surprise that I didn't have to fight someone, it was just the wind that was moving the tarp covering the slide. Who would have thought it? Well, new house, new noises, eh. After that adrenaline rush, we were slowly getting used to the noises of outside coming in, and we were not just ok with it, but I awaited with pleasure the sound of the rain on the roof, or the birds on a tree nearby.

After a while, I was sleeping even better than at home, not caring what was outside or where we parked. We parked and slept on many RV campgrounds where we had full-hookups of water, electricity and sewer connections, but many times when driving through we parked and stayed at many other not-really-RV parks. Walmart parking lots are known to most RVers to be welcoming spots in almost any state you'd be. The story goes that the Walmart founder was an avid RVer himself and always allowed RVers to park for the night at his lots. Some rules we learned early included parking at the back of the lots and trying to not make it a campground with chairs, blankets and/or BBQ grills out there.

If you respected them as a place of business, you were fine, and we parked at many Walmarts all around US. Another similar story goes with Cracker Barrel restaurants, where many even had RV/bus designated parking spaces. We parked often at them as well, went got some food and then to bed in their parking lot, ha. You do it often and you learn a couple tricks too, like not parking too close to their dumpsters as the trash trucks would come up super early (4-5am ish) to take their trash out. Not our favorite spots but we also did some truck stop areas or rest areas where overnight staying was allowed, as many rest areas don't allow overnight parking. Also, the truck stops typically have trucks come and go as the drivers get their 4-5 hours of sleep, and then move on as well as most of them running their engines or generators all night. We also stayed at state parks and other boondocking areas but not too many had the hookups to make it more than a few days' thing. The most impressing boondocking I recall was the driving toward Portland, Oregon on I-84 and it got dark and we had to stop for the night.

Julieth was already looking for spots where other RVers had mentioned they had stayed and was directing me to a gravel road right next to the Columbia River. Dark, rainy, and alone in the area, I park where she directed, disconnected the car just in case we wanted to move around quickly from there and went to sleep. The next morning, we woke up in one of the most beautiful areas by the river; we had hit the jackpot of gorgeous views of the river with its calmness and strength at the same time.

Parked next to Columbia River, Oregon

Working from anywhere

While we had the financial worst-case scenarios covered, it actually worked even better, as it usually does. I maintained a consulting gig with my prior employer and Julieth got to work for AARP, as a copyeditor for the Spanish version of the AARP website, all done online. While not everyone can work via the internet, many more service jobs can be performed offsite. It's just that many employers still don't trust that system, or haven't created a better system where they can hold people accountable and employees do not abuse it. Many more people are taking advantage of the situation, but there's still more that can be done. A good internet connection is key, and for us we had a Verizon hotspot that had signal even in areas that we didn't expect.

With a bit of self-discipline, this model can work for many more jobs and I believe the future to hold more of this off-site work for many employees. As for us, it allowed us to bring income, work from anywhere and enjoy our time whenever we wanted, as long as we completed our tasks.

Best discounts

Just because we were driving a thirsty beast averaging 8 miles per gallon, didn't mean we would just give up on economizing. After all, as a financial planner we should look for any and all financial benefits that we could take. We utilized many modern era technologies that wouldn't have been available to RVers even ten years ago. From navigation with real-time traffic reports to alternative routes with less traffic and thus less gas wasted, to using GasBuddy for our gas fill-ups, up to using certain RV-only discounts provided as a package when buying our RV. We had Good Sam Club discounts that would come handy at certain gas stations (like 'Flying J' or 'Pilot' Travel Centers for 10 cents off per gallon) as well as for RV parks discounts. We also joined 'Passport America' which would typically offer 50% off discounts at RV parks and we used that a lot.

Another one we used to save money as well as make new RV friends was 'Boondockers Welcome' where people in different areas that had available space would let fellow RVers park overnight for one or few nights for free, and some would even have some hook-ups, a great way to meet like-minded RV-stuff people and discuss road stories, interests and suchlike. We used it at times and met many good people that way, while we also learned new things about the area or RVing in general.

RVers are a very welcoming group, and very often they salute each other when passing just like bikers do, and not always but very often I would salute a fellow RVer especially if on a secondary road where we were driving slow enough to catch each other's eyesight.

Making a new friend – Joshua Tree National Park, CA

There are many excuses to not go on a road trip like ours, and one would be the cost of it. It is not cheap, but also you can make the best of it with less than you think. While many RV campgrounds charge on average $30-40/night or more, depending on where and the time, we would typically average $20/night by using discounts, parking at free lots, parks, Walmarts, Cracker Barrel and alike. If you want to find an excuse to not do something, you'll definitely find one, but if you'd like to make it happen, you'll also find a lot of ways to save money and have fun in the process.

Random stories

And fun we had, and some crazy stories to tell on a long wintry night over a big bonfire. Almost every day was something, but a few instances stand out from the crowd.

We got bees inside the RV in Florida and weren't sure where they were coming from. I looked at our Google maps and found out that we were near a bee apiary not too far from the campground. It was also springtime and we were parked near some really pretty flowers and I guess bees were mistaking our home for theirs. Who would have thought it?

In South Dakota, we picked up an unannounced visitor and gave him a ride across state lines into North Dakota. We were hearing noises behind cabinets, but thought it was the wind as usual, but not this time. A small mouse had snuck in and was hanging and driving around with us. We had to politely ask him to get off at the next station, which was a Walmart in North Dakota.

In Colorado, which we visited twice, we got snowed in, both times. On one instance, temperatures dropped in the low teens and we got our water pipes frozen. A quick drive at 2 am to the closest 24-hours store (another Walmart) and we got a small portable heater which we placed underneath on the storage compartments that slowly thawed the pipes without any damage, which would have been a big one.

We crossed US border into Canada where we were asked where we were going by the Canadian agent. When I responded we were heading to my brother outside Toronto, he was puzzled and asked, 'Why the RV?' Well, it's for the kids to see, or none of your business, but you know, have to be polite and all. On our way back we thought and read that we could even expect an inside inspection for 'illegal fruits and vegetables' or illegal Canadians, who knows, but when there, we were asked 'Anything to declare?' and a quick answer of 'No' saw us waved in with a 'Welcome back'.

Good thing they didn't check inside to see the twelve illegal Canadians—just joking, you immigration official, you! But over many other stories, I really enjoyed the driving, the knowledge that I was pulling the whole house and the responsibility that came with it, the driving in really tight areas and narrow roads, uphill and downhill, the acceleration, the braking, the turning of it, the parking, all of it. I was like a little kid at a truck store driving the red truck, wearing the imaginary firefighter hat. I loved it all.

Mail in RV?

For the three or four of you that are reading this in preparation for your own trip, your next question is about mail. Where do you get mail at if traveling in an RV like this? Great question, thank you. There are a few different ways to do that and there was some research that went into it too. Most full-time RVers either direct mail to a relative that agrees to get their mail and open it at times to see if important or not, or if you don't have such or don't want that inconvenience, there are businesses built around it.

First, you want to cancel any subscription that you don't want to receive any longer, and we did a few of those. Then you look for a provider that will give you a 'street address' and not just a P.O. Box. Many deliveries cannot be delivered to P.O. boxes, such as one using FedEx or UPS or even some official mail that needs to be mailed to an actual address.

We researched several providers and looked for reasonable prices of services, good software, as well as a local provider where the mail would eventually go. We went with anytimemailbox.com that had many locations that had partnered with it, providing a real street address, forwarding services, opening and scanning letters as well as unlimited online storage. Pricing was reasonable and our local provider was a nice family-run business that helped me several times with forwarding packages and letters to wherever we were.

Of course, I had no idea that such services existed, but this really facilitates the process of getting official mail, packages and more while you're on the go and yourself don't know where you'll be. There are several other similar services that certain RVers always on the go use even for residency purposes, such as in zero-income-tax states. Overall, a needed service to think about and much easier than bothering a relative of yours with your mail and other deliveries.

Where and how to sell it?

Just like most things in life, even the best ones, everything has an end. We were in California where we spent most of the following winter of 2018, and we visited Hawaii as well—of course, not with the RV— and now were debating about the final act, how to wrap it all up. The final act, as it happened to be, had nothing to do with RVing or financial literacy. Early in the New Year, it was the end of January 2018 when I heard a scream coming from the bathroom. It was Julieth, and since the bathroom is right next to the bedroom where I was lying, I got up fast to check on her.

She was crying, but I knew that was a happy cry not a sad one. She was holding a pregnancy test that showed we were pregnant. I was speechless at first, hugged her, and maybe a tear fell on my face as well. We were going to have a baby. We did one prenatal visit in California and now on the way back east we did another visit in Colorado.

Around March, we're right in the middle of US, in Kansas City, where we were discussing what to do about the RV. We liked it, but where to keep it since we live in a condo was a question, and expenses to maintain it heavily weighted on deciding to sell it.

Since we were almost middle of everywhere, I started the process of calling different RV dealers to see if they would buy it. After almost two weeks of keeping track of different people and dealers, as well as the prices quoted, the best price was offered in California.

I sent pictures, the VIN number and miles, as well as the model and we agreed on a price as long as it was in good condition as I described it. Now with the offer in hand and a 'virtual handshake' from the manager, we took the trip back to California, LA area, to sell our RV. This was a direct sale to the dealer, not a consignment where the dealer puts it in his lot to sell as I didn't want to deal with that and wait until it sold. Also, it was a huge improvement on the offers I received across the country. I got very low-ball offers from Michigan, Texas and even Florida, states known to have a high RV population, and the highest offer came from California. I guess there was an arbitrage opportunity between states, as the price difference from lowest to highest bid was over $15K, a big difference if someone doesn't do any research and just sells at his local 'friendly' dealer.

Knowing what I know now, the best place to buy an RV is probably Texas (the dealer we visited outside of Dallas) and the best place to sell is California. We also had the 'issue' of our personal items, kitchen stuff, the bikes etc. and how to bring them back to Baltimore.

We looked at different options on that too, renting a U-Haul truck and towing the 'little one' seemed like too many miles in a truck, plus we still had to park that and the Fiat at hotels etc. so that wasn't cutting it. We decided the best option for us was renting a U-Haul Box where you pack all your stuff in that big box and then it gets shipped anywhere in the country. We packed all our stuff, traveled to a U-Haul center in Kansas City and put all our boxes in the big U-Haul Box. Now all we had to worry about were some little personal items and the Fiat. We traveled all the way back to LA area, 1,700 miles and we did it in a week, as we weren't in a rush. At the dealer all the paperwork was ready, we just signed, someone took a quick look at the RV and that was it. The RV wasn't ours anymore.

We both felt sad, eating our lunch at the dealer's lunchroom and looking at each other like we did something wrong. But we didn't, we enjoyed it and we had the adventure of a lifetime, with another little adventure on the way. We spent couple of days in LA and then we took the cross-country trip back to Baltimore in the Fiat.

We stopped at a couple of national parks on the way (Arches National Park is gorgeous) and at a few hotels until after one week we arrived in Baltimore, tired but happy and in awe of what an experience it had been.

Adventure of a lifetime

Overall, our RV adventure was exactly that, an adventure that we will never forget. We maybe already forgot some details and hopefully this book will serve our memory, but we will never forget how it made us feel. Taking a break from the usual into the unknown is exciting, it enhances your senses and you can experience much more and in more depth. We visited almost all of US, which few people can say, and we did it our way, creating a path that is ours to keep and cherish. We saw things, beautiful things of nature, connected with it through hiking, walking, biking but also through just watching and wandering.

STANDUP

Hiking Mount Washington in New Hampshire

We hiked Mount Washington in New Hampshire, Pikes Peak in Colorado and biked alongside Columbia River in Oregon and picturesque Route One in California, amongst many others. We met new people, made new friends, helped people and got helped.

We helped many students with all their questions about money, about their debts, retirement options and how to even start thinking about it all. Their worries were big and their knowledge very limited, but at least we know we made at least a small difference in their thinking and overall knowledge about their personal finances.

We made memories that this book cannot capture, but at least will help us recall some of the wonderful times we had.

What matters is how and with whom you spend your time!
Grand Teton National Park, WY

Getting out of your 'box' is not just a good idea; it is almost mandatory to understand what's important to you and what you should value. An RV forces you to minimize your things and even your available inside space, but it opens up a much bigger whole world of wonder, outdoors, travel and adventure. During an adventure like this, you will get disconnected from what the current 'trend' is and into what's really important.

Spending time with people you love, connecting to nature, seeing and experiencing new things, opening yourself up to new connections, new people and new ideas and doing what you can to help others in need is what matters to me now. And it was all due to taking a risk, getting an RV, charting our own path & following that little voice that has always been saying, 'Just be you'.

STANDUP

Chapter 12

What's Next?

So, now what?

The pursuit of happiness is written everywhere, including the US constitution, yet most people cannot achieve it, are always in pursuit while looking hard on the outside at the latest gadgets, money, power, etc. to see if it will be there.

But even when they achieve those, they find out it's not there. Happiness, even if it comes from those outside factors, like money, power, gadgets, social media etc. is usually temporary and fleeting. Happiness is internal, how you feel with yourself, where you are and what you're doing. I also learned that your own happiness has less to do with doing stuff for yourself and more on doing for others. I've always had more satisfaction in doing things for others than myself, but this trip and this mission for others and increasing financial literacy in US made it even more clear. Your happiness depends on how you make others feel. It may feel weird at times thinking that your happiness depends on actions done to others, but it just works. Before leaving on this trip, a book was recommended by Josh Brown (a known financial advisor and #fintwit celebrity ☺) at a conference in Florida.

It was called 'The Go-Giver'. That little book reinforced even more our mission before embarking on it, that it is indeed what you do for others that determines your success. It was the final stamp of approval from the universe that we were doing something good for others as well as ourselves. Without giving the whole book away, but instead incentivizing you to read it, the book's main premises and key laws for success were about 1) how important it is to give more in value than take in payment, 2) how to always be authentic and be you, 3) how to serve as many people as possible and do it well, 4) how to place other people's interests first, and lastly, 5) how to be open to receiving as well. A simple book with simple premises but huge results if followed.

Also, according to many psychologists, happiness may not even be what it's hyped to be, and real fulfillment is achieved in finding meaning in life, doing and belonging to something beyond yourself. There's a great TED talk by Emily Esfahani Smith on finding meaning that has over 8.5 million views. She talks about the four pillars of finding meaning in your life, and I highly recommend it. The point, again, is that achieving that calmness and your purpose is typically found outside of yourself, in service and doing for others, either close family or complete strangers.

United States is a great country, but more than that it's an idea.

An idea of opportunity for all and anyone. It's just that some have more opportunities than others and a few do superbly better than most. My journey and passion for financial literacy comes from the idea that money is key to one's opportunities, and the more one knows on how to best get it and then manage it, the better the outcomes, the overall calmness and peace of mind. It is just that many cannot access this information, either because it's too complex, they're not interested as there are no immediate returns, or they just don't know where to start. It is at this juncture that a few interested and knowledgeable people can stand up and help out, share their knowledge, help others be better and start on a better financial path. I'm also of the belief that this knowledge of financial wellbeing expands much further than money, into relationships, stress, work performance and more. I'm biased on this, but I think the ripple effects of a more financially literate people are much bigger than personal finance or money, and expand into overall wellbeing, mindfulness, better care for oneself and another and overall a better country, hopefully less divided. Currently, many just live routine lives and in silent desperation, not knowing how to get to somewhere better, personally or financially.

I believe that financial literacy is a step closer to understanding what your time is being exchanged for, understanding your own worth, being educated and finally being more knowledgeable about your financial options and not taken advantage of. An expression out there is that 'being poor is very expensive', but what it should be is 'being financially illiterate is much more expensive' and increasing financial literacy will positively help someone get out of poverty in addition to other income-enhancing and training programs.

A call to financial professionals to StandUP

This book is a call for more financial professionals to stand up and do more, help out, share knowledge and help the majority of people to understand what we know, that getting your finances in order is a great achievement that gives you even more unexpected, beneficial side effects. It first gives you an understanding of where your money is going, and if it is being spent or saved in line with your values. Then it removes the ambiguity or the 'hearsay' from other people, when we don't know much. Lastly, it will give you confidence that you can achieve your goals, and you can finally achieve that calmness knowing that you will be OK. The real financial advisors need to stand up and be counted, really putting in their best efforts to make this happen, as serving just the top 1% or 5% of people won't cut it in the future. I even named my firm 'StandUP Advisors' thinking not just of myself, but a group of diverse advisors standing up and doing what's right.

The future belongs to those advisors who really open up their services, adopt practices to help more, put clients' interests first and provide valuable advice with no conflicts of interests. There are millions of people we can help and many more that don't even know what we do. The financial industry of only helping out the people who have 'already made' is the old model, which doesn't work and shouldn't work any longer.

This stuff is for everyone, and giving it to everyone and finding ways to share it and educate in your communities will give you back much more than you're giving. But don't even do it for the 'getting back', do it because it's the right thing to do, because you have information that can change someone's life for the better. Do it because the whole community and society benefits from better financial knowledge, and do it because you'd want it to be done to you if you weren't in your position.

At the very end, everyone thinks or reflects on what they've accomplished in their life, and you won't remember your AUMs (Assets Under Management), your performance reviews or your bonuses, but you will definitely remember the faces of people you helped and made better from your contributions. Don't wait to do that when you're old; start now and make that satisfaction last as long as possible.

Financial Regulators to do what's best for the people

But this book is also a call for the other sides of the 'Pentagon' I mentioned earlier to do their part in helping more people be financially literate, prepared and knowledgeable. It's a call for our financial regulators as well as legislators to put people's interests above their own or the financial lobby, to pass simple, easy-to-understand regulation that protects individuals from abusive practices, hidden fees and non-transparency.

People are confused and rightly so, as we have so many different titles to begin with, many using the 'financial advisor' title when they don't ever advise, but instead just sell financial products for their firms. The disclosures, that no one reads, are ever more complex and not in an easy-to-understand language, and many—when confused and fearful of being abused—take the easy road of doing nothing. And doing nothing, when you have nothing in order, is even worse. The regulators need to look out for the people and not special interests, but that could be a long shot.

Schools to start teaching financial literacy

Next, the learning institutions starting from high schools, or at times even earlier, and especially colleges should have a responsibility for getting students ready for real life after college. Financial literacy, especially at some critical times like prior to going to college or before graduating college, should be enhanced and reinforced so information that is relevant to that moment is made aware and current. A high school student getting ready to go to college would be best served with information on college degrees, careers to be expected, salaries and potential jobs as well as what the cost would be for this education.

Further information on how to pay for the school, besides the debt option should be explained and encouraged. Lastly, if debt is required, the costs, time and length of payment should be clear as well as put in perspective of a potential salary after college. While it cannot be 100% perfect, armed with this information, a prospective college student and her parents can be better informed and make better decisions.

While financial literacy should be reinforced during all of the college term, it's especially important to be enhanced and made practical when students are ready to graduate. It's at this point where I met most of the students on my trip, and they were anxious and full of questions about their future and money. It's at this time where budgeting and how to manage money comes in handy as they'll be getting their own money and job after many years of spending their parents' money (not always). They need to know how to save, where to save and how to start investing, after understanding what investing is and why it's important.

Employers to reinforce financial literacy and unbiased advice

The next phase that needs to change is at the employer. The employer has a responsibility to continue the educational, financial and overall wellbeing of his employees.

It is a benefit that serves the employees as well as the employer. Different researches point out that many employees lose time due to presenteeism (being at work but doing other non-work stuff) and worrying mainly about their personal finances.

A good employer will create a program with a local, knowledgeable, unbiased advisor or a financial coach to help these employees with their financial matters and provide either general & educational information or even better, individualized and actionable advice, to continue and be checked over time. This perk is seen to increase employee performance, morale and also loyalty, items that many employers are looking for and paying in either more money or other more expensive perks.

The individual responsibility needed for all to work out

Lastly, the individual should be made more aware of the benefits of understanding these for herself, as well as the negatives of not knowing these basic principles of financial knowledge. If all the parts of the 'Pentagon' are working together, and the individual sees the benefit of getting this knowledge, especially since for her benefit, that last piece will just fall in place. People, in different surveys, are either not aware of the value that a comprehensive financial plan will have for them since they don't have money now, or they think it would be too expensive or just haven't thought about it.

If we attack all the skepticism points, such as the why the urgency, how it could be offered at affordable cost, how it could be subsidized or even offered at work, or what the big benefits would be in starting now and for the future, the individual will be more than incentivized to go out and obtain such knowledge and take action.

Oh, and did I mentioned that improved health is another reason of pursuing saving and investing? Yep, in a study by Lamar Pierce, professor at Washington University, and Timothy Gubler, Ph.D. in Strategy from Washington University, they found that people who saved in their 401Ks showed improvements in their blood-test results and health behaviors 27% more than people who didn't save.

Maybe that stress reduction really does wonders.

A large movement starts small

Every small or big movement needs to start somewhere, and for me, financial literacy is the one that makes a huge impact on someone. If none of the other four 'Pentagon' pieces (regulators, schools, financial industry, employer) don't take any changes toward better financial knowledge sharing, for whatever reasons, there's always the individual that when empowered or well-informed can still overcome, learn and take action.

I'm just a small fish in a huge pond, but I've created resources that anyone can take advantage of and increase their financial literacy. One is this book you just read, and I've filled the above chapters full of financial knowledge that anyone can use and with which can take action. Second, I've created an online financial literacy course, **standup1.teachable.com**, that anyone can subscribe to and take in the comfort of their home or office. Third, I've created an online financial planning software that after a quick 15-20 minutes of inputting your household financial information, everyone can have a custom financial plan to start their thinking and planning right away. That's found at **standupadvisors.com/financial-plan**. Lastly, I've created several custom calculators on my website, standupadvisors.com, where everyone can go and calculate what investing periodically, or in lump sum, would look like, what waiting or paying high fees cost people, as well as what salary you'd have to make to afford your student debt.

These resources, free or at a reasonable cost, are the small contributions that I can make to the mission of financial literacy, together, hopefully, with the raising of awareness through my RV trip or writing of this book. It can be done bigger, I know, if more resources are put forward and more people involved.

During these last few years, I've met many like-minded people and advisors who are doing ever more in sharing, mostly for free, their ideas, resources, thoughts and knowledge with their thousands of followers. If you want to get an education in financial knowledge, just hang out on financial twitter (#fintwit), follow the right people, and you'll get to know them and learn a ton more and for free. But that's not for everyone, and for the ones that want to delegate and let an expert help them, do your homework and understand that not all advisors are created the same. Then hire a fiduciary who'll put your interests first.

What's Next?

You can make a difference

If you're thinking what difference would it make if you did something, think that even one person can really change the world. In many instances, we've let social purposes rest on the mercy of others (like charities) or on the power of the government.

Charities use persuasion, the good nature of people and tax benefits to raise assets needed, and the government uses the power to tax. There is, and if not yet in full force, should be a third way, a for-profit business that in the course of its normal business also solves greater social issues. Impact Investing (as it is now known) is coming more and more into today's lingo, but if we look deeper it has been going on for many decades, maybe not being called that. Jack Bogle, founder of Vanguard, died January 16th, 2019 at the age of 89. I watched people, many complete strangers to him, praise all he has done for the investing public, such as the fight to lower investment fees, and provide a way where people keep more of their returns, and not the intermediaries like financial services.

When he started this thought and idea, he was ridiculed by even his own peers. The Fidelity CEO at the time said that 'People don't want to have average returns' referring to what you get if you invest in index funds which as discussed often here, are unmanaged funds that follow a stated index. Now that same Fidelity, sure some forty years later, is on the forefront of lowering fees in the same index funds they ridiculed. Time changes people, ideas change and there's room for individuals to come up with their passions and change things too. All the major corporations, and even in school, all promote teamwork, but it is the individual with the crazy ideas who can and should change the world.

If you look about at all the people we remember who changed the world, they are all individuals, and behind large companies that made huge leaps in the world there are individuals. Think Mother Teresa, Ghandi, Mandela, Gjergj Kastriot Skenderbeg (Albanian national hero). Think Henry Ford or more recently Steve Jobs, Bill Gates, or Richard Branson; no matter who, they are all individuals with an idea, but most importantly the passion to follow through. The entrepreneurial path is a solo path until your idea is materialized and shows that it can work, then after that you get people as well as money, but you're all alone at the beginning. How you persevere during that start when nothing tangible is visible makes all the difference and separates the ones who move into the next phase of survival from the ones who don't.

The entrepreneur

Entrepreneurship is an exciting arena but with lots of defeats, stress, instances of depression and an overall psychological price. But like a gladiator in the arena, it has to be that way. If you want to revolutionize something, it can't be easy, as then either everyone would have done it, or the idea has no value to anyone. With Jack Bogle in my mind, it shows how perseverance and an idea of doing good while also surviving the business shows that just one person with an idea can and must change the world. I don't know of any team that changed the world, sure, maybe after the creator or founder got it to the place after its solitude, but let's think for a second. Would there be an Apple team without Steve Jobs, a Vanguard without Jack Bogle, a Virgin Group without Richard Branson, or a Microsoft without Bill Gates?

Maybe, but probably in a different version or maybe not at all. This entrepreneur at the center of it all is not my way of saying that it's all up to just this one person and the team is worthless. No, what I'm saying is that without that person that started it all, the company would not be the company it is now. Maybe it would be another company or maybe nothing at all, just not the one we know now, and for the examples I brought, the companies that are successful in changing people's lives for the better.

There's research on this too; known authors Todd Rose and Ogi Gas ran a project at Harvard known as the 'Dark Horse Project', studying all the very successful and unusual stories of people in a variety of fields. They also published a book called 'Dark Horse' where they detailed what they found out, mainly that people could find success doing things they were passionate about and that fulfill them. Many compare themselves to others and get lost and tired on such, but these 'dark horses' are super focused on being the best version of themselves, continuously self-improving and accomplishing things that matter to them, i.e. being themselves, and the rest just follows.

I am promoting this idea of the person and entrepreneurship not only because I believe it to be true, but because I want more people to take its path. Many will fail and many ideas are dead without even starting, but if a lot more people pursue this with the passion and drive (and hopefully a good idea) we will get a lot more in return to our society.

The third option of a business that promotes social good and purpose is the one that has better chances to survive than the one depending on charities of others or the one depending on the force of taxation. Jack Bogle, without even calling himself that, was a man with a social purpose and also a very unique business set up at Vanguard, where the company is owned by its funds, and thus the investors themselves. Many estimates put the number around $175 billion that his funds saved the investors since he started in 1974, compared to other funds many times as expensive. If you add, which you should, all the fees saved due to his company's pressure on the other companies to either keep up with their fees or lose business to Vanguard, that number runs easy into the trillions.

He saved people trillions of dollars, and in real life a dollar saved is more than a dollar earned, as taxes eat a portion of the dollar earned. Jack Bogle is the ultimate impact investing and shows that while a path full of 'deaths' and solitude, entrepreneurship offers the path to changing the world and society around you. He stood up for all of us 'little' investors when we didn't even know what to ask for and created a revolution that benefits millions of people even after his death.

And that is a worthy cause, to stand up and do something for others.

But you don't have to stand up for financial literacy or anything that you don't know or have passion about, but do stand up for the right causes that matter to you, doing what's right with passion and boldness. We know there are many problems in our society that need solutions, and may this be a call for all that can help to stand up, use their knowledge, experience and expertise and use it to better someone's life.

But first educate and help yourself, put yourself in the path to being financially independent so that you can be capable of helping others. My RV trip around the country and my story could just be a metaphor for the struggle that happens in you when you try to make a change and make a difference that you believe is in your long-term benefit.

As you read, it is not short of fears, adventures, and unexpected events, but it will also provide you with the lessons, perspectives and confidence to face the unknown, and in the process to become who you were meant to be. Just put yourself out there and do and be that person that is screaming inside of you. The universe will thank you.

So, what can each one of us do?

- Achieve your financial independence through education, planning, saving, and investing, then use your time to contribute back to your areas of knowledge and expertise. Be involved with likeminded people, working toward better systems.

What's Next?

- Embrace Uncertainty. Nothing is certain, as the experts don't know. We have some guidelines of what has worked in the past, but there are definitely no guarantees on the future. That's the beauty of life, it keeps you guessing and on your feet. Some hate the unpredictability of it; I say embrace it, love it, and make the best of it. Have back-up plans, two or three, expect it all. It doesn't make you uncommitted to the first plan.

- Think for yourself. See what rules you can come up with. And remember, the current rules were put in place by other people, and many not any smarter than you. If it doesn't work for you, just scrape it and make another one. Challenge it all. Put everything on the chopping block.

- Keep it simple. If anything gets too complex, start again and simplify. Start with your values and what's important to you. The first question to ask is 'Why?'

- Move from skepticism into activism. Do something that empowers others, help someone be better, and you'll be better too.

- The road less traveled is not for everyone, but the ones that resist through will find peace of mind. Find inner happiness, not by how many times you're 'liked' on social media, but how you feel when you're alone.

- If you really want it, you'll find a way, and if not, you'll find an excuse. You either live from a higher place with less stress and higher purpose or stay in the wheel of daily mundane routines.

- Appreciate what you already have and the road you've taken to be there. The journey is more important than the destination. And very often, the journey IS the Destination. Don't rush to get there.

- Pursue creativity, be creative, do public speaking, add & contribute rather than criticize or be defensive. Meet more people, especially if you're shy.

- Solve problems. There are many problems and we need creators, bold people with ideas to solve them. Be one of them. The future belongs to all, but some will give more and in return will also get more.

- Giving it all to others is the purpose. When you live to help others, happiness & meaning is always present. Others could be your family or close people, or people you've never met. But learn and take care of yourself first.

- Why do people with all with money & power get into philanthropy later in life? What do they discover? What if you started earlier? What if you said that there is nothing blocking you from giving now, your time, your effort, your shoulder, or your money, if you have any?

- Be the best that you can be, always be learning and improving, supported by a good system of freedoms, entrepreneurships, good network, education, self and formal education. Make a book about your principles – like this one or hopefully better.

- To the people who are able to do such, and have the freedom to help others when they can, this is a formal call to StandUP and be counted, fight for your beliefs, fight for the little guys who cannot help themselves, come up with solutions that solve current problems (even if unconventional, the market will show if they work or not). Don't ask for permission, just do it.

- And after you StandUP for others, that becomes your purpose, your fight, your light that guides you into something bigger than yourself. That is your legacy.

- The key is to live on purpose. I always ended my college presentations with: *The meaning of life is to find your gift. The purpose of life is to give it away* – by Pablo Picasso

- Lastly, be bold, creative & live with passion. This deserves a bit more…

Be BOLD:

In a sea of people, ideas and things that crave our attention, BOLD stands out, is different and calls for a moment of pause to appreciate. BOLD is not the same as CRAZY. Bold takes time, research, thoughts and dedication to perfect itself, to get to the right 'flavor' and to 'taste & smell different'. BOLD is also to lead ahead, even if people don't get it yet; most BOLD ideas are not well understood at the first stage, and even laughed at in the beginning, but BOLD is such as it doesn't get affected by those voices, and with confidence continues in the path of the unknown and the way where very few have passed before.

Be CREATIVE:

'Creative' comes from 'create', which is to make something.

As simple as it sounds, very few create, and even fewer are creative. The majority of us laugh, cry, enjoy, read, hear, watch, feel creations of others. Most of us consume.

We like, retweet, share, repost, and criticize much more than make, create, write, design, build, craft or invent.

Seth Godin, a known author and entrepreneur said it best:

The decline of our personal momentum might be the great untold story of our time. That electronic media, incoming, 'breaking', please reply, didn't you see that, react right now, click here... this has a cost. And the cost is our internal drive to initiate instead of to just react. Someone's driving. It's either you, going where you choose, or someone else, pushing you.

By creating, you're not only in a minority, but in the one group that has a chance to change course, to have an effect, to make yourself and other people feel happy, to reflect, to change lives. And by having that profound effect on others, you just created what's missing in many people's lives—your PURPOSE. Purpose to live, purpose to help, purpose to enjoy, purpose to heal, and purpose to love.

Live with PASSION:

The word PASSION comes from the Latin word 'Pati' which means 'to suffer'. Now why would you want to suffer? Again, most people would avoid 'suffering' and people don't go and look for it on purpose, but history teaches that suffering is the medicine, the 'click' that makes humans a different species, a soul that loves, that cares, that brings out the best in you. From the worst stories, there are stories of passion, compassion, empathy and love that strong they go through history and get told over and over again.

If BOLD is the 'how' and CREATIVE is the 'what', PASSION is the 'why'... The 'why' is also the most important one as it defines your purpose, your objective, your desires to live, help, love and be loved.

StandUP for someone, and one day, Someone will StandUP for you.

***

www.ingramcontent.com/pod-product-compliance
Lightning Source LLC
Chambersburg PA
CBHW050551160426

43199CB00015B/2620